Cherry Gilchrist began studying inner traditions in the 1970s. Her main lines of interest include Kabbalah, alchemy, astrology and meditation. After graduating from Cambridge University with a degree in English and Anthropology, she began a varied career which has included publishing, lecturing, music, running a Russian arts gallery and of course writing. She has had over 20 books published, including *The Elements of Alchemy* (Element Books, 1991) and a series of children's books on myth and legend for Barefoot Books. Her work often takes her abroad, especially to Russia, and she enjoys crossing between cultures, and exploring the links between ancient civilisations and esoteric traditions. Cherry has two grown-up children, and currently lives in the city of Bath, UK.

EVERYDAY ALCHEMY

HOW TO USE THE POWER OF ALCHEMY FOR DAILY CHANGE AND TRANSFORMATION

CHERRY GILCHRIST

RIDER

LONDON · SYDNEY · AUCKLAND · JOHANNESBURG

1 3 5 7 9 10 8 6 4 2

First published in 2002 by Rider,
an imprint of Ebury Press, Random House,
20 Vauxhall Bridge Road, London SW1V 2SA

Random House Australia (Pty) Limited
20 Alfred Street, Milsons Point, Sydney,
New South Wales 2061, Australia

Random House New Zealand Limited
18 Poland Road, Glenfield,
Auckland 10, New Zealand

Random House South Africa (Pty) Limited
Endulini, 5A Jubilee Road,
Parktown 2193, South Africa

The Random House Group Limited Reg. No. 954009

Papers used by Rider are natural, recyclable products
made from wood grown in sustainable forests.

Typeset by seagulls.
Printed and bound by Mackays of Chatham plc, Kent

A CIP catalogue record for this book
is available from the British Library

ISBN 0-7126-1574-1

Contents

* *

This is the Dragon devouring its own tail.

Prelude

* *

Ouroboros — The Sleeping Dragon

The practice of alchemy stretches back thousands of years. It was one of the esoteric arts of the Ancient Egyptians, who sought the secrets of transmuting metals. Later, seekers from Greek and Middle Eastern cultures recorded their visions of eternal gold, and added practical instructions for setting up an alchemical laboratory. During the Medieval period, the quest for turning base metal into gold spread into Europe. Alchemists could be found across a wide range of society, from ragged tricksters who promised instant gold in return for funds, to philosophic princes in Renaissance palaces, who shut themselves away in secret chambers to pursue the Great Work. And over in the Far East, there were yet other traditions of alchemy, which focused chiefly on the search for the ultimate medicine, the Elixir of Life, gleaming with the golden light of immortality.

The aim of alchemy is usually understood as the transformation of base metal into gold. Yet this can be interpreted in so many ways: historically, some historical alchemists certainly concentrated on the material properties of chemicals and metals, and their work in time gave rise to modern chemistry. This in turn then started to rule out the miracles and revelations that were so much a part of traditional alchemy. Other alchemists saw their path primarily as a mystical one, where developments in the laboratory were considered only an outward sign of divine transformation in the soul. But for most alchemists, spiritual and material labours have always gone together, and been expressed through the realm of imagery. The world of alchemical imagery is a fantastic one, teeming with winged beings, dragons and serpents, kings and queens, naked lovers and exotic birds and beasts. Imagery forms a kind of symbolic communication between the different levels of experience. For us today, it is just as important to span these different levels too. But rather than setting up a traditional alchemical laboratory, we can use our own lives as the prime material.

Alchemy is a living tradition, and has to be re-invented in each new age. However, connecting to the lineage of alchemists who have gone before us is important; the tree of alchemy has many branches, but they all connect to the main trunk, the tradition of transformation. There are ways of filling in the historical background; we have access to a vast number of alchemical tracts, which give us a wealth of imagery and enigmatic writings. Alchemists deliberately set out to mystify, so that 'the wise' might understand, and 'the ignorant' remain confused. They preferred to leave clues rather than recipes. But linking into the tradition is important, and one reason why I have chosen to illustrate this book with emblems from an important source, *Atlanta Fugiens* by Michael Maier (1617). Emblems formed part of the core material of alchemy, especially in the seventeenth century. The idea was based on Egyptian hieroglyphs, and the belief that you could contain a wealth of secret knowledge within one image, which only the initiated could truly understand. These complex, many-layered emblems largely replaced the more graphic alchemical woodcuts and illuminations from earlier centuries. The best emblem books were published in different languages throughout Europe, and became common currency for alchemists.

One of the most ancient symbols of alchemy is that of Ouroboros, the dragon or serpent which lies in a circle with its tail in its mouth. Within Ouroboros, everything is there in potential, but as yet, nothing has been realised; the dragon is asleep. And indeed, we already have everything within ourselves that we need for our alchemical journey. But first we have to wake the dragon. Then the aroused dragon must be battled with, and its three different energies released. The skill of alchemy is to combine these energies in a new way, so that they work at their highest potential. But, as the dragon says, 'In my beginning is my end.' And so the symbol of Ouroboros never loses its meaning, for in a sense, the journey is never completed; each ending is followed by a new beginning. Even if we eventually arrive back at the place where we first began our journey, nothing will be the same: all is transformed.

The presiding spirit of alchemy is Hermes Trismegistus. This is why alchemy is also often known as 'the Hermetic work'. The secondary meaning of hermetic as 'sealed' comes from the practice of alchemy itself, and relates to the closed vessel in which much of the transformation takes place. On a more symbolic level, this signifies that alchemical work is self-contained, and must be protected from intrusion. The legendary figure of Hermes Trismegistus is known as a master magician, the guide of souls, and also as a trickster figure. Although he is related to the Greek God Hermes, messenger of the Gods, he is a specific personification of revelation, wisdom and the arts of transformation. He is said to have initiated the first alchemists. *The Emerald Tablet of Hermes Trismegistus*, thought to have been written by the sage himself, became the key text for alchemists. It contains the famous saying: 'As above, so below'. The first known versions of this text appeared in Arabic in the ninth century AD, but its history may be far older. A version of *The Emerald Tablet* appears on page 108, Chapter 8.

Hermes himself has a life stretching back beyond recorded history, and certainly beyond the classical Greek myths where he was known as a trickster messenger and a charming thief. In his earlier incarnations, he was the god of boundaries, who carried a magical staff, and was also the mediator of quarrels, as well as being healer of the sick and patron deity of trading. His role was always that of a magical intermediary, and he could communicate even with the souls of the dead. From Greece, his cult spread to Egypt, and was then taken up in the esoteric culture of Alexandria, where Greek, Egyptian and Jewish traditions combined in the early centuries AD to form the Hermetic mystery schools. These included a strong element of alchemy. Hermes Trismegistus, meaning 'Thrice Great Hermes', was their guide, and many of the inspired writings of that period were attributed to Great Master Hermes himself. It is not surprising that later European alchemists also took Hermes as their patron, and aspired to follow his teachings.

Hermes Trismegistus is one of the chief sources of inspiration for *Everyday Alchemy*. His key symbol is the caduceus, the staff with two winged serpents winding around it. These represent the awakened energies of Ouroboros. The staff stands for the straight and firm direction of the work – our central aim of transformation. But on its own, it is not enough. There must be ways and means to achieve this end. The two serpents signify the ways in which we must be resourceful and even cunning, moving this way and that in order to reach the final goal. The caduceus thus stands for the taming and harnessing of creative power, the weaving of its three fundamental energies into a new and higher harmony.

As teacher and messenger, Hermes also shows us the importance of sharing with others any gains that we make. There are stories of alchemists in history who used their 'gold' (whether material or spiritual doesn't really matter) to help the poor and the sick. When alchemists succeed in making gold, they are expected to go further, and create the 'elixir of gold', which can then be used to make more gold. In our terms, this means that by transforming our potential into gold we create new possibilities which may be useful to others. We have a duty to bring these to life too. The caduceus is also a symbol of healing, and is still used as such over the doors of pharmacy shops today.

Everyday Alchemy is about making changes in your own life. It is also about celebrating life in its diversity, its fascinating detail, its possibilities for creativity and expansion. No book, of course, can do the work for you, and no book ever contains the complete key to transformation. The magic ingredient is you, yourself. You will not find instructions in this book on how to set up a traditional alchemical laboratory. What you will find is an approach which allows you to use your own experience as the material to work on. You are the alchemist in the laboratory of your life. Sometimes this will mean looking fully outward into the world, observing and participating in everyday life. Sometimes it implies going deep within yourself, and dropping the normal attachments of your waking self.

This book is not a completely traditional approach to alchemy, but it does move through the accepted sequence of alchemical transformation.

Alchemists wrote in a multitude of ways, and adopted their own interpretations of this sequence, but certain key stages come up in practically every version, and I have also kept to these. First of all, the basic
material, the *Prima Materia*, has to be identified and prepared for use,
however lowly or repellent it may seem to be. The secret of gold is that
its seeds are found in the most unlikely and primitive places. Then that
prime material must be processed, purified and cooked, opened up to
reveal its inner energies, steered through battles and reunions, killed
and resurrected, and finally turned into 'exalted' gold, also known as
the Elixir or Philosopher's Stone. You can find a more detailed description of the traditional alchemical stages in Appendix 3.

This book aims to provide a way of working for our time. It
springs from a tradition that I myself have worked in for many years,
but it is also a new stepping-off point. Like others before me, I have
created new material from traditional teachings; I have dipped my
pitcher into the age-old stream flowing from unseen lands, and as I
pour the water onto the ground, I endeavour to create a new rose-
garden of alchemy there.

Everyday Alchemy is intended to give the pleasure of wandering
through this garden; perhaps you will also discover there this
stream which has connected seekers down through the centuries. This
is the Stream of Knowledge, flowing through the ground of the
Common Life.

Using this Book

There are three basic ways of working with this book.

- As a self-taught course of work, following exercises given – ideally,
  this should be done in a group working together. Further suggestions for setting up and running a group are given in Appendix 1.
- As an adjunct to a tradition you are working in already, such as
  meditation, healing or divination – the exercises and insights
  should enrich the work you are already doing, and may suggest
  new approaches within your field.
- As a traveller's guide – the progress through the emblems and
  chapters can be taken as a guide to any type of journey, from

physical travel to the pilgrimage of life itself. You may have to work out interpretations for yourself, but if the chapters and emblems resonate with your own experience you will be able to use the book for inspiration, elucidation and comfort along the way.

In every chapter you will find exercises. Sometimes these are at the end, and sometimes interspersed among different sections. In the main text of each chapter you will find other starting points, which lead naturally to investigating your experience.

The exercises given are guidelines only, and if any should be unsuitable for you, you are at liberty to leave them. They are, however, designed to form a sequence, just as the alchemical process of making gold follows a course of development from the base material to the perfect metal. I advise following them in sequence if you can.

By doing these exercises, you are 'creating conditions' for something to happen. The exercises themselves cannot produce entirely predictable results. But they may initiate changes, stimulate growth, and help to unlock your creative potential. They are safe for practising on your own, or in a group, but please be careful. All exercises suggested here are to be followed in moderation, not obsessively, and should not involve excessive activity or deprivation. They may not always be comfortable, as they are designed to take us out of our everyday complacency. But neither are they meant as punishment.

Nothing can replace real live teaching. There is an old saying: 'When the pupil is ready, the teacher will come.' If you do not already have a teacher, perhaps working through *Everyday Alchemy* will help you to find one. Alchemy is for the independently minded; it does not require a guru figure, but someone who can act as a living guide, as your Hermes Trismegistus, is of inestimable value. This book itself is also more of a guide than a teacher. A guide shows you the terrain, walks with you through unknown territory, and reveals the view from the top of the mountain.

Take your time to work through these exercises; I recommend allowing yourself at least a year to complete them. Some exercises can be continued indefinitely. Some may require planning ahead to set aside a period of time to work intensively. You may want to overlap some of the sets of exercises, for instance continuing to work on an exercise from one set while you are beginning to explore the next set. No hard and fast rules are given.

Write down what you experience, and keep a record of your work. It is very easy to forget what you saw and learnt once you have returned to your normal way of thinking and seeing.

Take the egg and pierce it with a fiery sword.

Chapter One

❖ ❖ ❖ ❖ ❖ ❖ ❖ ❖ ❖ ❖ ❖ ❖ ❖

Cracking the Egg

This is the moment. You hold the sword in your hand, ready to pierce the egg that stands before you. It is the perfect egg, and the perfect moment to do the deed. Now is your chance to strike.

But it is terrifying to commit yourself to this moment. It is much easier to linger in the past or dream of the future. And the egg is beautiful as it is. If the sword doesn't strike cleanly, you might shatter the shell and damage the precious embryo of life inside it. Wouldn't it be better to leave it alone?

It is your choice, of course. The sword carries your intention, and you must decide whether you will use it to break open the alchemical egg and initiate the process of transformation. The egg may look perfect, but it is as yet undeveloped. From the moment of opening the egg, you must begin the work of developing the raw material it contains through every stage of change until it becomes alchemical gold. The egg will certainly perish if its potential is not released, so the choice cannot be postponed indefinitely. The gold you aspire to, on the other hand, is incorruptible. It is a symbol of enlightenment, the Elixir of Life, the realisation of Life beyond life, the Sun behind the sun. It is a place of safety for the human spirit, and an entry point into the divine world.

We can see from this emblem that the moment of impending change is frightening. The act of splitting the egg open will catapult the alchemist into an unknown world; from this moment on, he will be changed. He will have to leave his old life behind. On his face we can read apprehension, and even a hint of terror. But he knows that even though he trembles on the brink, he has to go forward. This chance may only come once in a lifetime.

There is also intense concentration in his expression. The perfect egg could be ruined by one careless slip with the sword. So his act of bravery must be carried out as precisely and skilfully as possible. As the accompanying verse says:

> *There is a bird, the most sublime of all,*
> *To find whose Egg should be your only care.*
> *Its white surrounds a soft and golden yolk:*
> *One cautiously attacks with fiery sword.*
> *Let Vulcan aid the work of Mars: the chick*
> *Hatched thence will conquer both the iron and the fire.*

Setting Out on the Path

Alchemy is about change. Each of us changes – life itself does that to us. Age, environment and experience affect us, altering our appearance and our outlook. Hopefully, we all finish our lives a little wiser than we started. But the work of alchemy makes different demands. It is for those who consciously seek change on a bigger scale – not change for change's sake, but for the growth of the spirit.

Alchemists have always said that there is a right moment to start the 'Great Work', and to initiate the alchemical process. They often advised choosing the time through astrology, calculating a moment with favourable planetary influences and at the right point in the lunar cycle. But perhaps more critical is the time that precedes that – the moment of choice, when the decision is made to undertake the work of transformation. Very often this can be triggered by a key event in life. In the sixteenth century, a young man called Jakob Boehme had a mysterious encounter. He was working as a humble and uneducated apprentice in a shoe shop. One day a stranger appeared in the doorway, his eyes burning with an unearthly light. He said: 'Jakob, thou art little, but shalt be great, and become another man, such a one as at whom the world shall wonder.' From that day, Jakob became aware of his destiny, and went on to become a famous alchemist and mystic. Was this stranger an angelic messenger? Such dramatic revelations are certainly not granted to everyone. However, many of us may experience something similar, so that even in ordinary meetings with normal people, words may be spoken that strike us with great power, and which become our divine imperative, urging us to take a different direction.

There may also be events in our lives which bring us to that moment of change. When I was a nineteen-year-old student, my boyfriend and I headed off to America for the summer. We bought an old camper van and decided to drive down through Mexico. One morning after a showery night, we were driving through the hills towards a little town in central Mexico. The surface was slippery and suddenly, as we were rounding a bend, the van skidded and veered towards the edge of the road. Below us was an almost sheer drop down a high earth cliff. I watched the whole process happen, and I remember thinking quite calmly: 'This is the last thought that I shall ever have.' I felt that it was a shame, but I was not frightened. Then the van plunged over the edge, and I fell with it into a kind of grey limbo. I 'woke up' after it had rolled over and over and come to rest at the bottom of the cliff. Miraculously, the two of us were almost unhurt, apart from bruises and minor cuts. But nothing was ever the same again.

For several weeks prior to the accident, I had sensed that something very frightening was about to happen, though I had no idea what. I felt that my world – my egg – was about to burst open. I would wake up at night in distress from nightmares, and yet I couldn't say what they were about. I decorated the inside of the van with cut-out stars and colourful cushions to try to make it feel like home, but I could not find any sense of security there. And after the accident, there was no blissful state of relief that I was still alive. In fact, we lived through a horrible period; to begin with, when we climbed back up to the road, no one would stop to help us although we were bleeding. When we finally got to hospital, we were treated and released within a few days, and then we had to live in the little mountain town for weeks while they sorted out our insurance claim because the official at the border had been too drunk to sign our papers. Our travellers' cheques had been stolen at the scene of the accident, so our money ran out, and we had to sleep in a hut where rats ran across the floor at night. I began to indulge in a fantasy that we had really died, and that now we were trapped in some kind of curious Otherworld.

By day, everything began to polarise into the good and the bad. There were good, kind people who helped us, fed us, and acted like Good Samaritans. There were also corrupt officials and those too callous to help. And the terror of the accident haunted me, as it did for months to come.

But – and here is the promise of gold among the dross – this event brought me to the most important choice of my life. I had come close to death, and I had to face up to this. I couldn't shelve the 'big questions' any more, about life and death and my own place on this planet. Back in the UK, I began attending a meditation class, and soon afterwards I found the particular line of work that I have followed until this day, which is rooted in the Western Hermetic and Kabbalistic tradition. The accident had shattered my world, but it brought new hope and a new way forward.

When the moment is seized, and the egg broken open, there is a real shift in life. It is like becoming a driver instead of a passenger. (Yes, I did learn to drive too, but I'm now talking on a symbolic level!) Your range of options increase – where to go, what speed to travel at, and what to see along the way. Of course, there are different dangers and responsibilities when you take charge of a fast and potentially lethal vehicle. The image is an apt one, as alchemy itself is often described as the speeding up of a natural process. Alchemy accelerates the work of nature, and the traditional alchemists often put themselves at serious physical risk in their laboratories, where explosions and escape of poisonous gases were common. You may be relieved to learn that, in this book, no dangerous laboratory experiments are recommended – we are taking the material of our own lives to work on. However, as an 'everyday alchemist', you may discover highly-charged areas of energy in your own being. This is still work that has to be handled with care and skill. As all the alchemists themselves have said, it also needs discipline, hard work and patience.

But the rewards are real. If you make the choice to change, you have the prospect of true transformation. To enter on the alchemical path may mark a major turning point in your life. But the beauty of alchemy is that it can be applied to great and small situations alike. You can create an alchemical change in your professional life or in your relationships, for instance; you can choose to initiate transformation by starting a study course, setting off on a journey, or beginning a new business venture. This doesn't mean that everything that we do in our lives is alchemy. For it to be true alchemy, you must make the change consciously, and be fully involved in the process.

You probably won't be reading this book unless you were already seeking some kind of change. What is it that you want to transform? Even if you can't describe it in words, you may recognise an urge deep inside you. Perhaps you have already passed the moment of decision, and are now ready to implement change. I've talked about making a choice, but this can often happen at a very deep level, almost without you noticing it at the time. Only later can you look back and say: 'Ah yes – *that* was the time that I chose to take this path.'

This sense of purpose and destiny is beautifully described in an ancient Gnostic poem called *The Hymn of the Robe of Glory*. It tells the story of a king's son, who is sent on a quest to find a precious pearl hidden in the depths of the earth. (In alchemy, gold and pearl are very closely related as symbols of perfection, and the goal of alchemy is often known as the Pearl of Great Price.)

The prince leaves his heavenly palace, and descends to this world, where he forgets his true origins and the task he has to perform. He goes to live in Egypt, which is a symbol for the dark land of sleep, and also, incidentally, for the 'black earth', the primal material of alchemy. His parents wait for him, but he doesn't return. So they compose a letter to him, and send it in the form of an eagle, the 'king-bird' and divine messenger.

> *It flew and alighted beside me*
> *And turned into speech altogether*
> *At its voice and at the sound of its wings*
> *I awoke and arose from my deep sleep.*

The eagle speaks the message to the drowsy prince:

Up and arise from thy sleep...
Remember that thou art a King's son...
Think of the Pearl
For which thou didst journey to Egypt.

So the royal son remembers who he is, and what he has to do. He finds the pearl, and begins the journey home. As he approaches his parents' palace, he sees the Robe of Glory spread out for him, which he receives along with the pearl of new wisdom and love that he has gained from his journey.

This allegory speaks to us all; we are all royal sons and daughters who have forgotten our heritage. Every one of us has a chance to awaken to the message of the eagle, and remember the mission we are on. But we become so immersed in the delights and desires of every-day life that we lose sight of our real destiny. And we have to make a conscious choice to fulfil it. We are given fresh chances; the message comes, often in an unexpected form, but we have to awaken to it. The pearl will lie forgotten in the depths of the earth, unless we remember to look for it.

Exercise 1: Following the Thread

What turning points can you identify in your own life? Review a crucial event, remembering as clearly as you can the outer sequence of action. You may feel emotional about this, but although you should acknowledge your emotions, it's important that they don't cloud the story.

Now put the event in context: what led up to it? Follow the thread back from the event itself. Try not to judge the reasons and causes, but just see what comes to mind. Then follow the thread forward. What changed as a result? Try to see it as a story, almost as though somebody else was telling it.

Write down what you have discovered. Repeat this exercise over the next few days, recalling the same event, and see if any of your perceptions change.

Overcoming Resistance

Look again at the picture of the man with the sword and the egg. There are clues here as to what the process of alchemy will involve. The fire is already blazing – a vital element, in which he will 'cook' the alchemical gold.

Behind the egg we can see the entrance to a tunnel. This has long been used as a symbol to represent the passage from this world to the next. Many accounts of near-death experiences report seeing a tunnel, or travelling down it. It is not only relevant to the border between life and death, but also as the entry point to other realms of consciousness. This is the crucial point where the known meets the unknown, and is usually guarded, to protect us from trespassing in a world we cannot easily cope with. Most of the time, we need our natural personal limitations in order to function as individuals. However, sometimes we may slip past the sentry; the person who ventures on to the alchemical path has to be prepared to pass over that threshold. In this emblem, the way is already open.

All this adds to the natural fear of opening the egg. Do you want the boundaries of your safe world to be destroyed? Resistance is only to be expected; it is a natural phenomenon, and we can find it in all beginnings and moments of change in our lives, great and small. If you keep something in the realm of ideas, it can remain perfect. If you decide to do it in reality, it will never fulfil your expectations exactly. And so it can be more pleasant to entertain an idea than to translate it into action.

Practically any project you embark on will generate its share of resistance, so it's worth getting to know resistance as a familiar old adversary, almost a friend. I travel abroad often, and the day before I leave I always regret my decision to go. It would be much nicer to stay at home. Why on earth do I need to go away? Come the next morning though, I'm ready for the adventure. And so I might as well not give too much attention to the suffering the day before, except to use it to galvanise me into completing my preparations and preparing mentally to make the break with home. Any creative activity also generates its share of resistance; I'm sure it was no co-incidence that I was ill for a week before I began to write this book. But because I have been a writer for many years, I recognise the syndrome. Knowing what it's about doesn't always magic the illness away, though sometimes it can, but at least I can face the beast. Oddly enough, this resistance sometimes lessens once I confront it.

Resistance does have its value, and it is a genuine force in the creative process. The positive, creative energy that wants to propel you into action has to be counterbalanced by another kind of force that can limit and channel it. The resistance helps to test out whether the idea is valid, and it modifies some of the dafter notions that we have in the heat of our initial enthusiasm. After creativity has met this containing, resisting force, then often a balance is struck between the two. If a deal is done, then the two forces work together to bring the idea to birth in reality. We shall see during the course of the book that you cannot get on without both these energies, and indeed without the very special third force, which creates the balance between the other two.

So acknowledge any resistance you may feel as part of the process. Listen to its grumblings and warnings courteously, but don't be put off by them. Let it temper your desires, but not extinguish them. Then you are ready to take that first step. It may be time to make a real change in your life. Or it may be the right moment to start a particular project, something that you haven't found the time or the willpower to begin before.

In one sense, the path of transformation involves a fresh start. But this doesn't mean throwing everything away. What you need to get going is already present; all you have to do is to use the ingredients in a different way, consciously and artfully. One of the secrets of alchemy is that you can use the most basic material to begin your work. Alchemists called this the primal material, or the prime substance, and described it as something rejected or overlooked. You do not need to search for magic ingredients in exotic locations; according to the alchemists, the necessary material can be found in our own rubbish bins.

The alchemists have always argued among themselves as to the exact nature of the primal material. Is it dust, dung, eggshells or urine? Is it earth or slime? Is it something more subtle, which cannot be described exactly? These arguments need not concern us too much, because we are not using physical substance in the traditional sense. If we are using ourselves as the alchemical vessel, and our life as the laboratory, then we must search for our 'prime substance' among our own experiences. Some people believe that they must go off to the Far East to find wisdom, or leave their jobs and families to begin their true quest. Alchemy says the opposite: begin with what you have, and work with it skilfully, consciously and imaginatively. This will produce true transformation. The Ouroboros, the sleeping serpent or dragon with its tail in its mouth, is the symbol of this unconscious potential. We have to wake it up.

> One is the All, and by it the All, and in it the All, and if it does not contain the All it is nothing.
>
> (*Gold Making of Cleopatra*, c. 100AD)

The quest to make gold in our lives is not an easy one. It can be difficult and painful; the alchemical process goes through a number of key stages, which involve battles and a kind of death and purification before the new life is truly born. It isn't a 'have it all' kind of philosophy. But it does offer us the chance to start from where we are.

When you start the process, you, the alchemist, must take personal responsibility for your actions. This does not mean nurturing delusions that the latest war in the world is entirely due to your bad temper, nor does it mean wallowing in guilt for your supposed misdeeds. It means acknowledging that what we do has consequences. We cannot always predict what those consequences will be, but we must be aware that our actions will generate results. If you take the steering wheel, you've got to do your best not to knock down pedestrians. And if you get stranded miles from anywhere because you forgot to check the fuel gauge, you can't blame anyone else.

You cannot predict precisely the outcome of your journey of transformation. If you practise astrology or divination, you will know that these reveal future trends rather than exact events. The symbolism of divination shows you in what kind of way things may work out, but rarely the specific future happenings. This is what makes life creative, and shows that we are not just automated slaves working to a fixed script. A person's will plays a large part, and the universe itself has remarkably imaginative ways of enacting those symbolic patterns. The journey that you take will certainly include an element of surprise.

Travelling on this path brings its own sense of security. But this is different from having complete control over it, or being immune to the kind of events that happen to ordinary people. Your confidence may be built up and broken many times. However, your faith in what you are doing will get stronger and stronger.

Exercise 2: Finding Your Will

Even habitual and minor actions have to be triggered by will; but will is not usually what we think it is. Try to see this for yourself:

a) Observe what in you initiates the process of getting up in the morning.

b) Choose another activity that you perform each day, such as washing-up. Look for the moment when you actually start it. Is it turning the taps on? Or did it begin a minute earlier, when you got up from your seat and headed for the sink? Was it a physical response, or a mental one?

Exercise 3: Initiating a Project

This exercise allows you to work on a small-scale, but in a similar manner to a complete alchemical process. It is not *what* you do that is important, so much as *how* you do it. Choose a short-term, not-too-ambitious project that you would like to accomplish. It could be a one-off event, such as giving a dinner party, or something with enduring results, such as mastering some new computing software. It can be as practical or as mundane as you like, but make sure it is something you can realistically accomplish and finish.

First formulate your intention in a simple way and write it down (eg, I am going to learn how to produce basic spreadsheets on my computer). Secondly, write down how long you need to complete this project, and what resources you will need for it. Thirdly, set a time to begin. Choose the time, and when it comes, make it a 'sacred moment' and clear some space in your schedule, even if it's only ten minutes. At this time of initiating the project, state your intention out loud. Then perform some appropriate first practical act (such as switching on the computer) to launch it.

Each time you come back to work on the project itself, begin by taking a moment to recall your intention and the space you created when you stated that intention.

Allow yourself some small act of celebration at completion. After you finish, note down your impressions and what you have achieved.

Sow your gold in the white foliated earth.

Chapter Two

* * * * * * * * * * * * * * *

Growing Gold

The poem for the image opposite says:

To the fat earth the farmers give their seeds,
After it's foliated with their rakes.
The Wise say, strew the gold on snowy fields,
Which have th'appearance of a flimsy leaf:
When you do this, look well, because gold grows,
Just as you see it mirrored in the wheat.

The idea of 'growing' gold is unfamiliar to us today. Gold can't grow in the same way that a tree or a plant can. And if you have gold already, as the emblem suggests, why do you need to try to make more? But it is not quite so strange as it sounds. Firstly, alchemical teachings were founded in a different world view, and secondly, these instructions are largely symbolic.

Although we now have a different understanding of the properties of metals and minerals, nevertheless the old alchemical views have much of interest in them, and are in some ways not too far from modern theories of evolution and consciousness. To the alchemist, the universe is a living, changing being. Everything in it is in a state of evolutionary growth, and traditional alchemy taught that all metals come to birth, evolving from base material into their final, perfect forms. Thus nature would ripen the seeds of gold over a long period of time until it matured. Unfortunately, nature would take thousands of years to do this, so the alchemists' work was to accelerate this natural process of transformation. In the early step shown in this emblem, the alchemist first separated out the 'seeds' of gold from the raw material, and then 'planted' them in the earth to initiate the sequence of growth.

Of course, you would not really expect to find an alchemist striding across a ploughed field carrying a basket of gold. Many, if not most, alchemists worked in a laboratory, and so the seeker would deduce that the 'snowy fields' did not literally mean farmland, but referred to the kind of chemical substance or compound that you would have to bury your 'primal' gold in. The seed gold itself was not gold as we would recognise it, but something that could grow to golden perfection if tended in the right way. Most practitioners took pains not to reveal their methods too precisely, so the aspiring alchemist had to try to work out what to do, often gleaning clues from other alchemical tracts.

Gold is the object of alchemy because it represents the pinnacle of creation in the natural world. In many cultures gold symbolises eternity, heaven and perfection. Even today, it continues to fascinate scientists. One of the latest theories is that gold as a metal was actually formed in a kind of furnace when two neutron stars collided, at a heat of a billion degrees. 'It's exciting to think that the gold in wedding rings was formed far away by colliding stars,' said one researcher as he explained his findings to his fellows. The imaginative qualities of alchemy have not entirely died out.

The question that continues to haunt us today is whether the alchemists ever really made gold. I raise it here not because I can give a definitive answer, but because the question, a difficult one, has to be acknowledged. Many people reject alchemy out of hand, because they assume that it was based on a delusion. I hope I've already shown that alchemy was understood on a spiritual as well as a physical level, and that taken as *the process of transformation*, it can be applied in different contexts, not just to the making of gold as such. So alchemy continues to have value for us today. But the traditional physical side of alchemy should not be dismissed either, even though it is beyond the scope of this book (see *The Elements of Alchemy*, Gilchrist 1991, and other recommended reading in the Select Bibliography). It is possible to make gold by nuclear fission, and the frontiers of science are never fixed; things that seem impossible to us according to today's understanding may be explained by tomorrow's research. It *may* be possible to achieve minor miracles by patient, repetitive and conscious work, and thus producing changes in physical substance that cannot be accounted for in normal scientific terms.

It is fair to say that the physical and chemical framework used by alchemy has been updated, which is why it is very difficult for anyone today to work in a traditional alchemical laboratory, but it is *not* fair to say that the alchemists achieved nothing. As I hope this book will show, the principles embedded in their work are as vitally important for us today in terms of our lives as they were hundreds of years ago. So for the purposes of *Everyday Alchemy* we will not venture too far into the dark recesses of the alchemical laboratory as it traditionally operated, but rather follow the thread of that teaching into the hidden chambers of our own lives. The alchemists searched for the seeds of gold in their prime matter; we shall search for them in our life experience.

Many aspects of alchemy helped to pave the way for modern scientific method, and the devoted attention paid by the alchemists to their experiments later turned into the techniques of precise observation that are now standard laboratory procedure. But whereas scientific method tries to strip away personal involvement and 'human error', alchemy works in a different way. The conscious participation of the alchemist is the essential fertiliser for helping the process to develop. Watching the stages of the alchemical transformation unfold was not only the means of charting the process, but a thrilling experience for the alchemist, looking into the secrets of creation. The epigram bids us to '*look well*', and in those two apparently insignificant words lies one of the prime secrets of alchemy: *Give attention to what you are doing.* Attention acts as the magical 'third force' operating to connect the material experiment and the psyche of the experimenter. It is this that helps us to achieve real transformation, and we will come back to this third ingredient again and again in the book.

The work at this stage is to find the seeds of gold, and plant them in specially prepared earth with full attention. In due course, a golden harvest can be reaped. Practising alchemy in everyday life is the opposite of living mechanically. It is about committing yourself to growth, and working consciously. Because it is *not* a mechanistic science, you cannot be absolutely certain of the outcome. Where the forces of change operate, you do not know exactly how things will turn out. This is another great difference between alchemy and modern science, which aims to replicate experiments exactly. Alchemy is a journey, and an adventure.

Alchemy affirms the view that there is a life force that carries the most humble and unpromising material forward towards ultimate perfection. If we recognise this process, we can learn to work with it in our own lifetime; we can transform our own being through these efforts.

Where Are the Seeds of Gold?

The seeds of gold are hidden already in our own life experience; we don't need to wait for someone to bring us the magic ingredients. There's no need to search for the pot of gold at the end of the rainbow. If we look within the texture of everyday life, and in the storehouse of memory, we can find plenty of primitive gold to work with. In the first chapter, we began the work of turning over the ground and investigating past experience. Memories have to be recovered in a truthful form; we have to dig into past episodes to release the meaning buried there.

'Meaning' is in fact one way of defining the seed of gold. Meaning connects us to joy and purpose in life, and it is this joy of life that can grow from a small seed into a golden tree. But 'meaning' is not exactly the same for everyone; my sense of meaning will be different from yours. It doesn't matter whether it is large or small, and it doesn't have to be of world importance – John Lennon once remarked that keeping a house full of budgerigars is a perfectly good way to contribute to life if it has meaning for you. Difficulties can be faced if we can find meaning in them, and the humblest forms of work can be satisfying if they are meaningful to us. We need gold to grow gold because that love of life is needed to develop our individual destiny – the work we do, the contribution we make and the relationships we forge. A person who has lost touch with the source of that love is in a truly desolate situation. As the tree grows, it raises its branches and leaves to the sky, receiving the 'heavenly dew', as it is known in alchemy, and digging its roots deep into the core of life below.

For many of us, confused by the demands of daily work in a highly pressurised society, and jaded from the bounty of goods and pursuits on offer, it can be hard to sort out the gold from the dross. Sometimes a crisis will show us quite clearly which aspects of our lives have meaning to us. A few years ago, I discovered a lump in my breast. It turned out to be harmless, but during those few days before I had the tests, I felt as though I was about to be thrown off the train of life. I really saw this in my mind – the brightly-lit carriages full of happy people continuing their journey, whereas mine was about to end. But this crisis also showed me exactly what I wanted to keep going with. Work that I had often complained about now seemed infinitely precious to me, whereas other aspects of life that had seemed important, I knew I could dispense with. Since then I have kept faith with that knowledge, and it has helped me even at times when I have felt like giving up my work.

Seeds of gold are often to be found in an interest that once gripped you passionately, perhaps when you were much younger. It could be something to do with sport, music, or nature, for instance. Maybe you rejected this interest later in favour of more adult or fashionable pursuits. Maybe someone mocked your interest, or you became too competitive and lost your natural pleasure in it. Often the hormonal upheavals of adolescence, or the demands of bringing up a young family, simply push our treasured interests to one side. They may be dumped in the personal rubbish bin, but are still lying there waiting to be reclaimed, glistening with promise.

Of course, you have moved on, and old delights probably need to be upgraded. But if you can re-establish contact with one of them, you have a real seed of gold that can still germinate and grow. We may learn to be more sophisticated, but in doing so we can cut ourselves off from this simple genuine love of life in one manifestation or another. There is no growth of 'golden fruit' without that love. You can observe this in people who have an incredible intellectual grasp of a subject, but no real connection with it. You would not trust them with your confidential problems because they do not seem to have an emotional 'body', and you would not expect any truly creative work to come from them. However, meet a gardener who knows about roses, and works with roses, and you will find yourself enthralled at what he can tell you, even if roses are not your thing. The chances are that you will also be able to apply what you learn in a different context.

A developed person is not someone who has lost their particular interests, but a person who has embraced them. This means taking a delight in Creation, and sharing common ground with others. Beware of the so-called spiritual teacher who has no hobbies, and claims to be beyond the warp and weft of everyday life. Even the most advanced people have their interests. It is a touchstone of our humanity. J.G. Bennett, a teacher in the Gurdjieff tradition, used to study under one of Gurdjieff's followers, Pyotr Ouspensky, who was a formidable teacher in his own right. Bennett was greatly in awe of Ouspensky at that time, and when the revered master asked him to find some antiquarian prints, Bennett regarded it as a great test. He successfully tracked down the engravings.

> When I told Ouspensky he was delighted, and asked me to go with him… I spent the afternoon [with him]. He thoroughly enjoyed himself, bought a number of prints, and said he would go again a week later. He invited me to tea, which he made with great care from special Chinese leaves he had personally selected at Twinings. I was ridiculously stiff, not realizing that Ouspensky was a human being who enjoyed human companionship.

I know a Buddhist teacher who breeds Tibetan terriers for a hobby. I also met a Benedictine monk who adored sailing, and who was occasionally granted leave to do just that. It wasn't a selfish pleasure, because the joy he felt in this also manifested in the love and kindness he showed towards visitors to his abbey.

For a monk largely removed from the 'worldly' life, any such breaks and activities might be especially cherished. This joy in life, the seed of gold that we are searching for, may be easier to identify when we have less, rather than more. Many of us are seduced into endless shopping and accumulation of wonderful gadgets, yet this doesn't always generate as much genuine pleasure as some of the simpler activities, such as taking a walk through the woods, or brewing home-made beer.

A friend of mine went through a deep depression, even though she had all those things in her home and family life that are supposed to make us happy. She had somehow lost the sense of what it all meant. For a long time, she was despondent. Then one day, when I visited her, I noticed that she had dug over her garden, and planted a beautiful array of flowers and shrubs. As soon as I saw this, I knew that she was on the road to recovery. She had done it with love and attention, and by committing herself to tending this growing garden, she was also generating new growth in herself.

Whatever point you are at on your path, you may sometimes need to renew your connection with life. This will lead you into a new cycle of transformation. There are smaller cycles and greater ones, and in one sense, every moment offers a chance to renew and begin again. No one can force you into the journey of transformation; it's your own will that starts you off. It may be a struggle to find this desire at times, but if you do, it will help to renew your zest for life.

This zest is neither greed nor self-indulgence. It is more like a re-discovery of the Garden of Eden, in which there is still room for inno-cent love and where you have eyes to see the beauty of the world. Once, on an intensive study course, we had to live for several days in darkened rooms without any glimpse of the outside world. When we were finally allowed outside, I felt as though I was stepping into Paradise. I saw the green of the leaves and the colours of the flowers, and I smelt the grass and felt the warm sun as I had never done before. I suddenly realised that this was my birthright; I might forget about it, but I could always return to it, and no one could take it away from me.

Exercise 1: Finding Gold
Can you find the gold in your life? If you had to give up everything except for one task, or one commitment, what would that be? It may be small or large, humble or high-profile.

Exercise 2: Testing the Gold

Look back through your life, and remember what moved you, engaged you, and inspired you in the past. Have you neglected any of those activities since? Could you possibly resurrect one of them? If necessary, make the decision to try one of them out again, if only for a day. Be prepared to treat it light-heartedly!

Exercise 3: Preparing the Snowy Fields

The 'snowy fields' referred to in the emblem represent a field of consciousness, which acts as a fertile seedbed. It can best be prepared by using your attention. We usually cut down the flow of impressions reaching us, and reduce the wealth of sensory input that we could receive, but you can focus your attention by using your senses as widely and fully as possible.

What can you see? What can you hear? What sensations do you have? Can you smell anything? What kind of a taste is in your mouth? Can you feel the breath passing in and out of your nostrils? Try to sense what is behind you, as well as seeing what is in front of you. Do not interpret or try to change what you experience, just give it your full attention.

Practise this twice a day for five minutes, and it will have a noticeable effect. Don't be tempted to extend it beyond those five minutes, at least until you have had a lot of experience with this exercise, or you could find yourself in an uneasy kind of half-world as normal activity tries to take over. However, doing the practice may in any case have the effect of alerting you now and then during the course of daily life – waking you up, as it were, out of your normal preoccupations. Be ready to respond if this happens by calmly extending your field of awareness for a minute or so.

One word of warning: you might be tempted to interpret these 'wake-up calls' as an alarm signal that something is wrong, but this is unlikely. You are simply becoming more aware of the transition between the normal daydreaming state and being fully awake in the moment. If in doubt, just extend your senses and remain quietly observant.

Meditation

The miracle of alchemy is that you can work with what you have. One of the best ways of keeping the 'white field' fertile is through regular meditation. However, a regular meditation practice has to be taught, not learnt out of a book, although we will look deeper into certain aspects of meditation in Chapter 9. It is never too early in a course of personal development to take up meditation, and if you are ready to start, some contact addresses for reliable teaching organisations are listed on page 173.

Tending Your Seedbed

Now that you have the primal gold, and some fertile ground to plant it in, you can begin the process of tending its growth. I have suggested that it must begin with a love of life, and we have looked at ways of fostering this. Don't forget that you can make a deliberate decision to do something that you are not in the mood for. If you feel bleak, then deciding to go out for a walk, and giving your full attention to what you see around you, will almost certainly help to lift your mood and renew your sense of meaning. In the longer-term, taking up an activity that you do purely for pleasure, not for its profit or usefulness, can also help to regenerate a healthy connection with life. Exercising the senses will keep the connection alive and provide a good foundation for the growth of that seed into a golden tree.

Then comes the active 'gardening', which at this stage means doing what needs to be done. This might sound faintly absurd, but in fact most of the time we *don't* do this. We run on automatic pilot, using routines and habits to help us navigate through daily life. If we can start to train our observation, however, we may perceive more clearly what is really needed. Observation is more focused than attention, the basis of active consciousness. Attention stays broad, whereas observation can concentrate on one aspect at a time. It is possible – though not easy – to practise both at the same time.

A woman I was visiting suddenly got up and went to fetch her mending kit. She had observed that my sandal strap had broken off, and she sewed it up securely for me. She did what was needed, irrespective of the fact that we were not close friends and did not even have any great liking for one another. Because she focused on this need, it came across to me as a significant act of kindness, and though it happened over twenty years ago, it is still fresh in my mind.

Another woman I knew lost her husband very suddenly from a brain tumour, when he was still only in his thirties. When I went to her home, I wanted to try to make myself useful. To be honest, I was at rather a loss to know how to console her. So I asked her what needed to be done. She hesitated, then showed me to a dark and dreary basement, and asked me if I would mind clearing out his work files and papers, which I did. To my surprise, I heard later that this had been a great support to her at a critical time. Actions speak louder than words, and these incidents suggest that their appropriateness determines how significant they are, not the amount of time they take. And giving true attention to such actions will help to turn them into gold.

Perhaps all this seems a far cry from the hidden, secret world of alchemy. But this approach does have a magical effect. Even if you were to take the process of transformation no further, you would find that following the practices outlined in these first two chapters would leave you refreshed, enthused, and with more creative ideas at your disposal. Later on, we will touch on more obviously exciting work with visualisation and inner journeys. But these would only produce superficial results unless the process of real transformation were grounded in everyday life. However, there is one exercise that I would like to introduce here. It takes a while to establish, but it is an important exercise, which helps to sort out the threads of experience and memory. We will return to this exercise later in the book.

Exercise 4: Remembering Backwards (Part 1)

To be effective, this exercise must be done every night when you go to bed for at least a three-month period. It will start to undo the editing process that goes on in your mind, and it may also over the course of time unlock old memories and change the content of your dreams. Because of this, you might find it helpful to keep a dream diary from the time that you start the exercise. You should not expect immediate or dramatic results from the practice, though some people find it does make their dreams more vivid.

Just before you go to sleep, go backwards in your mind through everything that you have done today, starting from this moment in bed, then travelling backwards through the day. For instance, see yourself as you got into bed; before that you were in the bathroom; prior to that you were coming up the stairs; having a last cup of coffee – and so on. Follow the thread, but only according to what you can genuinely remember and picture. Do not try to reverse the actions themselves as you would if you were re-winding a film; you should review them as little sequences. In other words, see yourself climbing up the stairs, not moving backwards down them. Go back through the day, and through the previous day too, as far back as you can before you fall asleep. In fact, you are quite likely to fall asleep while you are still reviewing tonight's teeth-brushing in the bathroom. This doesn't matter at all.

When you have the white lead, do the women's work, that is, COOK.

Chapter Three

. . . .

Washing and Cooking:
The Patient Alchemist

In this emblem we see a simple sixteenth-century domestic scene. A pregnant woman is cooking in a spacious kitchen. A cat crouches nearby on the floor, perhaps poised to catch a mouse, while on the far wall dishes and spoons are arranged neatly in racks. Through the open window we can glimpse a view of a road leading away through open countryside. But although this is a peaceful, everyday scene, note how powerfully the elements are present. Water, fire and air are much more involved in the cooking process here than in our modern homes. For a start, the woman is cooking over a large open fire. A pot of boiling water is suspended directly over the blaze. Bellows lie on the hearth to fan the dancing flames. Beside the hearth, wood is to hand to feed the fire, while under it some form of coal is stored for more sustained and steady heating. Fresh air rushes in through the unglazed window, and the draft creates a huge, swirling cloud of smoke and steam, which must somehow find its way up into the canopy of the chimney. Water is also present in a tub of water on the floor, where two fishes are swimming, probably waiting to be boiled alive.

The woman is an alchemist. She deals with the raw and transforms it into the cooked. Even her pregnancy is a form of alchemical transformation, the gestation that is nurtured in the warm waters of her womb, gradually creating new life. She presides over all this with gentleness and poise. Each alchemical stage contains a challenge: hers is to control the elements with patience and skill. Notice the look of keen concentration on the woman's face – she may be serene, but she is not in a dream. She is alert and utterly focused on her task. She is ready to temper the fire at every moment.

The 'white lead' referred to in the epigram is the alchemist's term for tin. This shows that we have travelled on from the earlier stage of working with the dull, black lead that was sometimes used as the prime material in alchemy. Black lead is a symbol of Saturn, the spirit of heaviness and melancholy.

> *Whoever wants with ease much to achieve,*
> *Should scatter snow on Saturn's face ('tis black):*
> *And you'll receive the whitest stuff of lead,*
> *So then remains to you but women's work.*
> *Then COOK it like a woman heating pans,*
> *But in its water let the TROUT dissolve.*

This apparently humdrum picture is full of symbolism. Look at the careful arrangement of the wood into three and two pieces. The three probably stand for the three components of alchemy – salt, sulphur and mercury, also known as the three forces of transformation, and standing for the body, soul and spirit of the Work (see Appendix 3). The two may represent fire and water, the opposites which must be united, or they might be the black and white lead already referred to. The cat crouching on the floor – could this be the playful, fleet spirit of Hermes, mastermind of alchemical manipulation? And why is there an empty, overturned bucket under the sink, near to the un-shuttered window? Perhaps it signifies that the way is open, and that the process has begun. Everything is carefully placed, and every detail has its meaning. Even the arrangement of four pots on the hearth probably stands for the four elements. Although Maier's emblems are especially finely drawn, it's typical to find this type of symbolism embedded in alchemical illustrations, particularly of the sixteenth to eighteenth centuries. In them lies the code to the philosophy of alchemy.

Alchemical images are powerful, and have an archetypal quality. There are many accounts of alchemical imagery turning up in dreams, sometimes even when the person concerned has never read a word about alchemy, as the psychologist Jung noted. Although no two alchemists wrote or drew alike, similar motifs recur. The two fishes that we see in this emblem appear in another alchemical work of the period, *The Book of Lambspring*, and the poem written there sheds light on what they might mean:

> *The Sages will tell you*
> *That two fishes are in our sea*
> *Without any flesh or bones.*
> *Let them be cooked in their own water;*
> *Then they also will become a vast sea,*
> *The vastness of which no man can describe.*
> *Moreover, the Sages say*
> *That the two fishes are only one, not two;*
> *They are two, and nevertheless they are one,*
> *Body, Spirit, and Soul.*
> *Now, I tell you most truly,*
> *Cook these three together,*
> *That there may be a very large sea.*

So in the emblem we are exploring, even this minor detail of two fishes swimming in a tub contains a wealth of secret knowledge. Everything in these images is worth contemplating. What, for instance, is the large sea referred to in the poem above? It is far more than a mere instruction on how to cook the fish. Its deeper meaning may be reflected in the following ancient text from the early centuries AD. This is one of the 'Hermetic' writings ascribed to the legendary teacher Hermes Trismegistus, a body of knowledge which was passed down through the lineage of alchemy.

> *Tat* (the Seeker) – Tell me then, father, why did not God impart mind to all men?
> *Hermes* – It was his will, my son, that mind should be placed in the midst as a prize that human souls may win.
> *Tat* – And where did he place it?

Hermes – He filled a great basin with mind, and sent it down to earth; and he appointed a herald, and bade him make proclamation to the hearts of men: 'Hearken, each human heart; dip yourself in this basin, if you can, recognizing for what purpose you have been made, and believing that you shall ascend to Him who sent the basin down.' Now those who gave heed to the proclamation, and dipped themselves in the bath of mind, these men got a share of *gnosis*; they received mind, and so became complete men.

(from *Hermetica*, Book IV, ed. Sir Walter Scott)

So this sea may be 'the bath of mind', in which we have a choice to immerse ourselves and thus receive our birthright and fulfil our destiny.

Cooking – Is It Really Alchemy?

Alchemy combines the ordinary and the extraordinary. It encourages us to be bold in bridging the worlds between material and spirit, and it uses imagery to help us cross to and fro. For the traditional alchemist, the point of action was in the secluded experimental laboratory. For us, it is in the theatre of everyday life. For both, the real fruits ripen in the soul.

Strangely enough, cooking is a very good way to appreciate how alchemy works. It is one of the best processes of transformation that we have in everyday life, and one that we can put into practice ourselves. Remember that no alchemy is complete without conscious participation. If I talk about transformation through cooking, the obvious results will be on the physical level – producing something good to eat. But for alchemy to affect us, we have to engage with that process. We need to give it our attention, even when the work is repetitive. This way, the transformation can proceed at every level, not just in the saucepan.

So what is transformation? The word comes up again and again in alchemy, so we need to try to penetrate its meaning. Here is a simple example from the humble kitchen; but it is true alchemy.

A few weeks ago, I decided to make some bramble jelly. It was late summer, and the days were sunny and mellow. There is a patch of wild blackberries just over my garden wall, and I picked and ate them practically every day, often just stewing them up with apples. Then I wanted to do something different with them, to keep the flavour of summer berries in my store cupboard through the cold months of winter ahead. I followed the recipe by cooking the blackberries in water, then straining them overnight through a canvas jelly bag. The slow drip resulted in a litre or so of a clear, dark liquid, to which I added sugar and then boiled up. The temperature is crucial; first it must be gentle, to dissolve the sugar without burning it, and then brought up so that it is high enough to reach the 'setting point', the temperature at which the jelly will set. Some jellies and jams will be ready in a few minutes, while others take up to three quarters of an hour. The cook must be very watchful, because it's impossible to predict exactly how long it will take.

You must also pour it into warmed glass jars before it sets completely. If the jars are not warmed, they may crack. If the jelly is taken off the stove too soon, you'll have a runny mixture, and if you leave it too long it will become too rubbery and the flavour will alter. (If it was completely straightforward to make preserves, there would not be so many jam-making competitions in this country!) Fortunately, in my case the result was a translucent jelly, of a beautiful dark ruby colour. The pots stand in my cupboard; the berry has been transformed into a new substance, but the jelly nevertheless retains the beauty of the blackberry, and the delicacy and tang of its taste. And this jelly can be kept for months, unlike the berry that rots so quickly on the bush.

Bramble jelly became my triumph of domestic alchemy, the 'gold' achieved from three simple ingredients – berries, water and sugar – and transformed through the agency of fire. The jelly contains the essence of blackberry. The berry has lost its original form, but through this sacrifice, its essence is released and is embodied in a new and purer form. In alchemy, the death of the 'body' must occur, which then liberates the soul and spirit; these in turn find a home in a new 'glorified' body. Later in this book we will look more closely at this period of darkness, when all seems to be lost before the new life reveals itself.

It is extraordinary to think that the humble blackberry and jelly-making can be seen in such mystical terms, but true transformation has taken place. Transformation is a change of state, a process by which the whole person or substance is changed. Transformation is not a change of outward appearance; a hare whose coat changes from brown in summer to white in winter has not really been transformed. But a caterpillar goes through a real process of transformation to become a butterfly.

Cooking is a creative process. Cooking transforms the ingredients, whereas 'food-fixing', on the other hand, simply combines them. With cooking, although we may have a result in mind, such as making a cake or a mayonnaise, it is still an unpredictable process and there is an element of risk that something will go wrong – the mayonnaise will curdle or the cake sag. The end result depends largely upon the individual quality of the ingredients and the skill of the cook. Science may say that results can be replicated if you start with exactly the same ingredients and work in exactly the same conditions. But when is this ever possible? Who can fully predict the final taste of wine that is being made? The variables, such as the weather conditions, the state of the soil and so on, can be assessed to some extent. But perhaps there is more to it than that. After all, no one grape is ever *exactly* the same as any other grape. No two people are identical. The very fact of existing at a different point in time and space creates differences between people, plants or raw materials. Astrologers argue that where and when a person is born will define his or her character. This is not perceived as a simple causal effect, but is tied into the view that the Cosmos itself has a conscious life.

This whole Cosmos… is full of Life. And there is nothing therein, through all Eternity, neither of the whole nor of its parts, which doth not live. For not a single thing that is, or has been, or shall be in this Cosmos, is dead.

(*The Divine Pymander of Hermes Trismegistus*)

The opposite view, which has only been prevalent for a couple of centuries, is that nothing in the universe has consciousness, apart from humans and animals. The picture that this conjures up, of isolated little drops of consciousness existing in a vast, bleak Cosmos starved of any life or meaning, is really very peculiar. At the forefront of science this picture is now changing, but to all intents and purposes our modern society is founded on it, the legacy of mechanistic science and the Industrial Revolution. We should not reject it entirely, because every viewpoint has certain possibilities, and most of us are glad overall to have cheap goods, swift means of travel, and agriculture which does not depend entirely upon hard manual labour. These are the direct rewards of an understanding of mechanisation. But there is a price to pay as well; on the spiritual level, it has resulted in a struggle to retain faith in religion or even to acknowledge the sacred aspect of life. On the physical level, it has brought us a legion of ills including road accidents, weapons that are destructive on a large scale, and the pollution of land through intensive farming.

Cooking has also found a place in factory production, where easily prepared meals can be manufactured for our increasingly rushed and stressed population. Commercial cooking has largely followed the creed of science, so that in theory we are guaranteed identical tastes in convenience foods. I wonder about this. It often seems to me that one can of baked beans does not taste quite the same as another. Strangely enough, just after writing this paragraph I went downstairs to feed my two Maine Coon cats, Rufus and Pushkin. I opened a tin of their normal brand of cat food. To my alarm, it didn't look right at all – it consisted of brownish water swilling around some rather evil-smelling lumps. I decided to put it to the feline test. The cats sniffed at it from a distance, and wouldn't even approach it. Then they pestered me till I produced something more acceptable. I expect there was some 'rational' explanation – perhaps the machine that stirred the vat wasn't working properly – but it shows that consistency still can't be guaranteed, even by factory production. Everyone knows the best cars aren't made on Friday afternoon or Monday morning, and I for one will never again buy a sofa made just before Christmas when the work force are celebrating.

It's impossible to follow the path of alchemy and hold the view that the universe is completely mechanical. Alchemy shows us a world where body, soul and spirit interconnect and influence each other. This does not mean that there are no laws operating; in fact it's very important to try to understand the principles upon which this interconnected Cosmos functions. And technique is not derided; the alchemist must be skilful and precise in his or her work. Perhaps alchemy is well-suited to today's world because although it is not an easy discipline to understand, it does combine the elements of creativity, technique and principle in an approach that spans all levels of existence. It is neither purely mystical nor purely physical, but could be described as a sort of 'super-science' which includes the worlds of both consciousness and materiality.

The old forms of alchemy have to be re-visioned, however. We cannot retreat into the world of alchemy that existed before empirical science was born, even if alchemy itself helped to give birth to that science. But if we want to survive spiritually, we have to embrace the idea of a living Cosmos. Alchemy doesn't demand that you belong to any specific religion. Historically, it has found followers in Ancient Egypt, Greece, China and the Moslem world as well as in Christian Europe, so it is plainly not tied to any one faith or creed. But it does demand that we explore the world of spirit, being willing to acknowledge our own experience in this realm rather than explaining it away.

Exercise 1: Transforming Ingredients into Food

Everyone can cook, even if it's only in a basic way. If you think you can't cook, perhaps now is the time to try. Choose something to make that really results in a transformation of the raw ingredients, such as apple pie, lemonade, strawberry jam, meringues or mayonnaise. You can use a recipe if you need to. As you cook, give the process your full attention. Use all your senses: watch, listen, taste, smell and touch. Notice your own technique in action and the different processes you have to use. If you are using heat, pay particular attention to the way you control this and the way in which it affects the ingredients. When you have finished cooking, go over the process in your mind. Do you feel it was continuous, or broken up into little sequences? Did you notice any sudden shifts when the composition of the ingredients changed?

Moments of Change

Transformation is not limited to the kitchen. Look about you and you will soon begin to notice other examples. Some of them may be very practical or specific processes such as a tadpole turning into a frog, or glass being made from sand. But there are also activities where transformation suddenly takes place when you reach a certain stage. Let's say you pass a building site every morning on your way to work. At what point do those steel girders and slabs of concrete suddenly become a building? This is the moment in which it acquires an identity as a place, and is no longer merely a collection of building materials.

For some years, I have run a business selling Russian arts and crafts. Before I opened a gallery, I used to take them around to fairs and exhibitions. Set-up is exciting, though pressured; there is a moment when the untidy pile of boxes on a table changes into a real display. This happens before everything is finally in place. Taking the display down is not so pleasant, in my experience, as you destroy your day's creation. Nevertheless, there is a moment of transition during the downward cycle of transformation too. There is a specific point when the objects on the table are no longer a display, and it's fascinating to try to catch this moment.

There is always energy at the point of transformation. These points are like little births and deaths, and people are very attracted to these 'liminal' moments. Any stallholder will tell you that there is often a buzz of interest as the display is about to take shape, and, more irritatingly, just when it is being taken down.

Humans have an instinctive understanding of transformation, and take a natural delight in it too. Conjuring shows are always popular, where magicians apparently turn silk scarves into rabbits, and make coins appear out of thin air. Small children have the luxury of believing that this really happens; as adults, we know that such things are not literally possible, but the tricks remind us that, nevertheless, we live in a magical universe where transformation is possible.

Even for adults, though, it can sometimes be hard to know which tricks may be genuine – for example, the possibilities of mind-reading, spoon-bending, and so on, are accepted as real by most people, whereas sleight-of-hand tricks with cards are fascinating but are based on creating an illusion. The philosopher Gurdjieff put on stage shows in which his pupils performed both kinds of stunts, where some feats were performed simply by trickery, and some genuinely used psychic powers. The audience could not tell which were which. In repressive societies, anything that appears to be magic, even if it is purely practical, can get the practitioner into trouble. In the sixteenth century, the English academic John Dee was nearly imprisoned for constructing some wonderful stage machinery that included a giant beetle that could actually 'fly'. Members of the audience denounced him as a sorcerer. John Dee was in fact also a magician and an astrologer, but ironically on this occasion he was simply using his considerable talents as an engineer and inventor.

Not all apparent magic is real. Perhaps we should be on our guard against an apparent promise of transformation, which may be dangled enticingly before our eyes, but is in reality fraudulent. Advertising plays on our desire to transform our lives, our appearance, and our image in the eyes of others. It too works through imagery, so that although an advertisement cannot legally tell lies, it can create a fairy tale, a fantasy, and an atmosphere that will seduce us into believing its implicit promise of transformation – if only we buy that car, perfume or coffee.

We long to transform our lives, but the caution we know we should use with advertisements also applies to a developmental teaching system. Beware of anything that sets out to appeal to greed, love of power or vanity. Good spiritual teachers never promise enlightenment or material benefits as a result of practising their teaching. Rewards and results cannot be guaranteed, although these teachers can open our eyes to the possibilities of following that path. Nor will they make claims for themselves. In the meditation classes I attended, the teacher was often asked by his pupils if he himself had attained enlightenment. Gently and slowly he would always reply: 'If I say "Yes" – what will you think? And if I say "No" – what will you think?'

Of the following exercises, three are practical, so you may choose to space these out time-wise, or even just select one of them if you have limited time available.

Exercise 2: Observing Transformation
Look around you for examples of transformation. Watch what happens in nature, look around your home and workplace, and observe your own activities. Keep to external examples, and don't choose processes of inner personal change. Record what you observe: what is the transformation to and from? Is there a different word that describes the before and after identity, such as caterpillar/butterfly or construction site/building?

Exercise 3: Inner Changes
Try to identify some of the key moments of transformation in your life. These may not be so much the dramatic events of life as the times when you knew something had irrevocably changed. What had changed? Take out some old photos of yourself, creating a sequence from babyhood to the present moment if you can. Where do you see the different phases beginning and ending? What do they signify? How much do they relate to physical changes (such as puberty or menopause) and how much to life events?

Exercise 4: Creative Transformation
Now set yourself a task which will bring about transformation. It should be something practical and which you have a good chance of achieving within a reasonable time limit – certainly no longer than a few days. (If this works, you can always set yourself a giant project later on, such as erecting a mini Stonehenge in the back garden.) The criteria for transformation need not be too strict; it could be redecorating a room, for example. The important thing is that the task should result in visible transformation that you yourself can appreciate. It could involve building, assembling, decorating, forging, re-organising, displaying or anything that takes your fancy. Once again, observe the process. Try to see where the moments of transformation come.

Exercise 5: Creating Something from Nothing

This exercise is about using discarded materials creatively, and shows how there is plenty of potential within the Prime Material.

Search among your discarded waste. Look through any rubbish that you are in the process of throwing out, through scraps of material, or through boxes of bits and pieces left in the garage or tool shed. Take three or four items and make something with them. It can be decorative, useful or simply weird. It's up to you.

If you prefer, you can turn this into another cooking exercise. Have a look in your kitchen store cupboard. Choose three or four ingredients that you hardly ever use – but make sure that they are still fit to eat! Think about each one – what it is, what it can do, and its essential taste and characteristics. Then invent a recipe with them. Even if it isn't very edible, it will be creative. But you may surprise yourself by producing something truly gastronomic.

Exercise 6: Changing Lives

This exercise is for fun and to stretch your imagination. If you could transform yourself into another kind of being, what would it be? Jot down a description of your new exalted state, your appearance, and what you can do.

*The Wolf coming from the East and the Dog coming
from the West have bitten each other.*

Chapter Four

Into Battle

The wolf and the dog are close cousins, yet here their violent antagonism towards one another overrides any sense of kinship they might have felt. Snarling and slavering, they fasten their teeth into each other's throats, drawing blood in the fury of the fight.

There is no alchemy without conflict. The Ouroboros, the coiled serpent that represents the whole process of alchemy, contains everything in potential. But it must be awoken for that potential to be realised. The duality which lies dormant has to be released. Alchemy uses many different images, such as fire and water, sun and moon, dog and wolf, or man and woman, to signify the polarity that must be identified, then provoked into battle. This battle is not aimed at ultimate destruction, but rather to generate energy and bring about a new union.

The Wolf comes from the sunrise, but from where
It sets there comes the dog, both wild with rage.
Now each one bites the other, bites in fury,
Their muzzles gaping in a rabid snarl.
These are the twin stones, freely given you
In all things and at all times; grasp them well.

In alchemy, some of these pairs of opposites have their own particular significance, such as the green lion and the red lion. The green lion represents the peaceful, perpetual spirit of Nature, content to turn the wheel of life steadily and to change gradually. The red lion symbolises the rampant energy that wants action right now, the fire of alchemy that generates sudden change. Both are needed for transformation: the patient repetition and reflection of the green lion must combine with the surging, provocative energy of the red lion. They can be released from the first body of matter in alchemy:

> I am the poison-dripping dragon, who is everywhere… My water and fire destroy and put together; from my body you may extract the green lion and the red.
>
> (*Aurelia Occulta: Theatrum Chemicum Britannicum,*
> ed. Elias Ashmole, 1652).

Thus they are also related to water and fire, the two elements that it is essential to combine in alchemy, however difficult this task may be. We'll look further into the meaning of red and green in alchemy further on in the book.

The same process has to go on within us too. We have to identify the conflicting elements at work in our lives. The very act of recognising those conflicts will help to release energy. In fact, we don't usually have to look far to find battles already raging in various corners of our internal empire. It can be painful to acknowledge conflict; alchemy is not a peaceful practice, and you may sometimes feel that you are in the grip of forces beyond your control. No one comes through real change without discovering those raw elements within themselves. We may begin alchemical work in the hope that it will give us some control over the troubles of everyday life. In a sense it will, but not by cutting us off from them. But alchemy is skilful; it contains the battle, and aims to produce a constructive outcome with the minimum of damage. Battle is not the objective; it is a part of the process.

Find the Worm

In this and the next two chapters, we'll follow the arousal of the sleeping Ouroboros, which leads to the awakening of desire, the ascent of passion, and the winged flight of the soul. These stages can be described using a set of four symbols known as the Worm, the Sea Serpent, the Dragon and the Angel. They form a framework in their own right, leading from basic instinct to the operation of higher intelligence. They are also in one sense the four manifestations of Ouroboros awoken, already inherent both within the sleeping serpent and within our own sphere of life. Just as Ouroboros has to be aroused and 'processed' through stages of transformation, so we have to awaken our knowledge of Worm, Sea Serpent, Dragon and Angel, and learn to work actively with these levels of being. In this chapter, we will focus on the Worm. It is the first manifestation of the awoken Ouroboros, rather lowly and somewhat sluggish, but actually very powerful and deeply significant in our lives.

The Worm represents the fundamental life force that keeps us ticking over. Its prime mode of operating is through desire or repulsion. Both of these are fundamental triggers for conflict if we can't or won't follow its dictates. The Worm responds both to external stimulus, and to internal changes in our body state. Its job is to keep us going, ensure the reproduction of the species, and protect our individual identity. (As our little individual Worm is really a part of a larger Species Worm, this leads to some conflicting demands, as we shall see.) The Worm lets us know if we are hungry, or cold, or sexually aroused. It works through our most primitive responses, which can sometimes be uncomfortable. I have always known, of course, that hunger and pain can be intense sensations, but I had no idea that we are also acutely responsive to stimuli such as light, until one night I was woken up suddenly when the bedroom light was turned on. My reaction was not far short of pain; I dimly realised that I was trying to squirm away from the light, just like a worm. I felt a kind of primitive anguish as my body sought the darkness that it needed.

You may catch the Worm at work when you wake up in the night, or perhaps after a daytime nap, and you feel disorientated. If I sleep in the day, I often wake up with an urgent desire to eat something sweet. Is this a basic need to boost my blood sugar, or could it be a throwback to infant days? We do sometimes tap into that infantile level of being, experiencing sensations that can be both powerful and uncomfortable. Those sensations can arise in dreams, such as the dream of being stuck on one's hands and knees, desperately trying to stand up, but pulled back by the forces of gravity. This is surely a buried memory from the time of learning to walk.

Children are closer to the 'Worm' level than adults. This means that they are, strangely enough, more dispassionate. They often experiment coolly in a way that we find horrific, such as pulling the wings off flies. The 'Worm' does not have much concept of the suffering of others. Nor do children place any extra meaning on their own pain, for they experience it for what it is. They don't prolong their response. The baby is driven by hunger to cry lustily, alerting adults to its very real needs, but when milk comes the crying soon stops. A young baby lives more fully in the present than any of us. This state carries on into the early years of childhood; when a small child falls over and howls, the reaction lasts only as long as the painful sensation does. It has not yet learnt to feel sorry for itself, to worry about injury or to blame others. But gradually, the child learns from the adults around that an awful lot more can be packed into the experience, and it is worth crying more to express wounded pride, or to get more attention and comfort from a parent.

Just as the child does not at first think of pain as evidence of an unkind world, so the first things they do that hurt others are without any cruel motive. When I was about three years old, I tried to stuff our new kitten into a cellophane bag. My father punished me, and I learnt my lesson: you don't do this to live animals. But I also remember my own shock at this punishment, because I had had no sense of causing distress – I just thought the kitten would fit rather neatly into the bag. But afterwards, I felt bad about what I had done. This wasn't merely a response *learnt* from my father's reaction, but more as though I had woken up to the suffering I had caused. Conscience, like the sleeping Ouroboros, has to be awoken.

This has an interesting implication – that children are born with an immediate, self-centred 'Worm' response to life, but that experience triggers awareness of others. Through bumps and bangs, reprimands and rebuffs, the child learns that the Worm cannot act out all its desires, and through these too the individual human conscience is stirred. Early conflict awakens our latent faculties.

The Worm doesn't go away, however sophisticated or old we grow, and it is very apparent if we experience intense physical pain. This can turn any of us from a rational human being into a writhing worm. However, ultimately pain is a response designed to protect the organism, so the Worm is only doing its job. If we feel pain, at least we are alive. It can be helpful to remind oneself that 'pain is only pain'. Often other fears or sorrows fly in like bats to roost, and they attach themselves to the pain with tenacious claws, making it far worse than it might otherwise be. Acknowledging the pain for what it is without its entourage of woes is useful.

The Worm also operates in our reproductive urge. It is voracious in its desires; a woman may physically ache to have a child. And the Worm has no idea of logic or reason. Another woman may have a carefully constructed life plan which officially rules out conception for another five years, but – what a surprise! – she 'accidentally' falls pregnant. Accident or Worm at work? Many of us assume that we can override all these natural urges in favour of other goals. We can – but only up to a point. 'The worm will turn' is as good a saying as any; we can deny its power for a while, but any urge denied for too long has a habit of rearing its wormy head at the most inconvenient moments.

The Worm reveals itself through revulsion too. This often takes an apparently irrational form, such as disgust at hairs in the plughole or a horror of spiders. It can be hard to work out which of these reactions are instinctive and inborn, and which are socially created. Some may be rooted in our survival instincts, alerting us to dirty conditions or dangerous creatures, but others may be learnt; one society, for example, finds it perfectly acceptable to eat insects, while another is revolted by the idea. More importantly for our purposes, aversion and desire are two sides of the same coin. But their poles can reverse. Many successful novels have plots built around a hero and heroine who begin by loathing one another, then find that this is really a powerful attraction after all.

Knowing the Worm puts you in touch with the kernel of life. We can learn from it what are our true, inbuilt needs that help us to survive, and what are the more conditioned desires, which may or may not be so useful. The Worm, if we learn to listen to it, can inform us directly of our *real* physical needs, not what we *think* we need. We learn that there are times when we can override Worm desires, and other times when we do so at our peril. Contacting the Worm connects us more directly to the flow of energy that keeps us going. By teasing it out of its hole, it becomes a faculty that we can consult when needs be.

Discovering the Worm

Exercise 1

Be aware of the moments when you wake up, and see if the Worm is operating. What sensations does it give you? What does it want?

Exercise 2

Next time you feel physical pain, however slight, be ready to observe it. Strip away all overlay of hurt feelings, fear or frustration. What is the pain in reality?

Exercise 3

Take one simple physical thing that you find repellent, such as an insect or a kind of food, and find out what happens when you deliberately put yourself in contact with it. Can you observe it clearly, without letting the repulsion dominate? Do not suppress any conflict you experience during this contact, but allow it to play itself out. Then ask if there is anything about it that you actually find attractive. Can you find the seeds of desire in that repulsion, and even reverse it to a positive attraction?

The Roots of Conflict

Conflict arising from human interaction can sometimes be more painful to live with than physical wounds. It can release powerful emotions, and often the battleground ends up being inside us. I once had such an internal battle, in which I struggled against the poison of pure jealousy. A man who I was friendly with at the time deliberately taunted me at a party by turning his attention to another woman and ignoring me. I was so possessed by the pain and venom of jealousy, that I couldn't sleep for the whole night. I had no claim on him, and so there was nothing I could do without making myself look ridiculous. Although this episode was not very important in terms of the bigger picture of my life, it touched a raw nerve at a bad moment. However, I learnt one important thing from it: I never wanted to be in the grip of that particular emotion again, because it was so consuming and destructive. But such relatively minor skirmishes that leave you sore for a few days can help to prepare you for times of real trouble. Years later, when faced with the break-up of my marriage, this experience came in useful. I realised that if I gave way to responses fuelled by anger or jealousy, I would damage myself more than the others involved. I decided to concentrate on rebuilding my own life, rather than becoming bitter and vengeful. I needed my energy; I couldn't afford to waste it on such negative emotions.

There is no hard and fast rule as to when to keep a battle to yourself, and when to fight it in the outside world. The main guideline is to fight it with the minimum force possible, and to use its energy as productively as you can. Conflicts need not always be bad news; they generate energy that can be channelled. Once I was at a concert listening to a piece played by a trio of young musicians. All three were really throwing themselves into their performance, but something a little strange was happening. The two young men were playing fervently, even ostentatiously, while the beautiful blonde lady cellist showed nothing but complete composure. The greater the men's energy, and the more intensely their music soared, the cooler the control that she exercised. The impact, musically, was phenomenal. 'What's going on?' I whispered to a neighbour. 'Oh,' he replied, 'they're both in love with her. She's taken up with one of them and dropped the other, so they're fighting over her.'

Some people stir up conflict deliberately in order to generate the energy required for something else. In another musical context, I once knew a professional singer who was famous not only for his fine voice, but for his quarrelsome nature which always peaked on the day of a concert. He would pick on something – a wrongly made-out bill, his girlfriend's cooking, the lateness of the bus – and launch into an offensive. This was the way he roused his own energy to put into his performance. It may not have been an ideal way to operate, and he had a high turnover of girlfriends, but it certainly got him singing well.

Conflict is inevitable. Just being alive creates conflict. We each have to occupy a certain amount of space simply to exist, which means that someone else can't have it. If two of you want the last seat on the train, there is a conflict of interests, however politely you handle it. Apparently one of the easiest ways to get yourself killed in Africa is to stand between an advancing hippopotamus and the river. It has no concept of going round you. You constitute a challenge because you are occupying the space that it is set on passing through.

We affirm our existence and identity with every breath – even taking a breath slightly enlarges the amount of room we take up! Horses know a good trick; they blow themselves out so that the girth appears tight and the saddle securely in place. Then they let all that air out again when the rider tries to mount, so that the saddle slides round and deposits the unfortunate person on the ground. Even a small, assertive extension of body space can have a significant effect!

Just as on a physical level our body fights off viruses and infections to maintain itself, so on a psychological level we try to avert attacks on the beliefs and feelings which form part of our identity. Social etiquette provides for this; we tell people that their awful cooking tastes wonderful, and that their lurid choice of wallpaper is 'most striking', rather than hurt their feelings by giving our real opinion. We often avoid conversations about politics or religion, partly so that our own views do not come under attack. If you start the day with a newspaper, the chances are that you choose one that confirms your own outlook – unless, that is, you are like the singer described above, and want to give yourself an early morning boost of fury. Society encourages us to skip around these confrontations, and to create a mechanism for achieving common consent, so that the wheels turn smoothly. But in alchemy, we have to face up to conflicts. They are a place where we have to use courage but at the same time temper our reactions.

One way of processing conflict is to include it in our rites and customs; another way, sometimes combined with this, is to treat it playfully. If you look closely at certain types of dances, especially traditional forms of folk dance, you can see all kinds of actions that resemble fighting, even in simple movements like slapping hands with your partner, or approaching an opposing line of dancers as if they were the enemy. Martial arts are often learnt through a gentler and more playful form of combat; we talk about 'sword play' and there is the 'Tai Chi Dance', Tai Chi being a slow and graceful version of a Chinese fighting form. The element of playfulness fits in very well with the alchemical concept of Hermes, the playful trickster, whose artful cunning helps to find solutions where the two adversaries are locked in combat.

This is also reflected in the way that conflict is often ritualised. While not playful in the normal sense, conflict can involve a kind of 'play-acting'. There have always been codes of honour which govern wars, such as the obligation to treat prisoners well and to respect flags of truce. This can help to avoid an outcome of ultimate destruction, which is in no one's best interests. Animals rarely fight to the death if they are not planning to eat their opponent. By using warning signals, they can often avoid a fight altogether. You can watch a pair of cats spending hours disputing their territory without ever touching each other, through a complex ritual of aggressive posture, vocal threats and slinking submission.

Many battles are about settling disputes without destroying the opposition. This reflects the sense of common life that we share. There is a Buddhist story about a man who planned to murder a fellow passenger on a train. He thought out every move, and followed his intended victim to the corridor, ready to push the man out of the train door. He got the door open and was just about to give him a shove, when suddenly the train lurched forward. Without thinking, he grabbed the victim to stop him toppling out. His instinct to save a fellow member of the human race had prevailed over his murderous intentions.

Conflict is not all about destruction. In fact, channelled conflict can be creative and productive. It can release energy, and change repulsion to attraction. It can stimulate excitement, sexuality, laughter and heightened experience. The boundary between battle and sexual engagement is indeed very narrow. Courtship rites both in animals and humans often involve a certain amount of sparring, and a repeated pattern of quite aggressive advance and rejection that lasts until the final rebuff or acceptance.

Exercise 4: Handling Conflict

For one day, pay particular attention to every conflict of every type that crops up in your life, whether it's personal, public, professional, physical, psychological or practical. A conflict may be small, like asserting your rightful place in the bus queue, or it may be a major argument with your boss. As each one arises, try to see what the two poles of the conflict are. If the conflict is between two people, are you the dog or the wolf? The dog, for instance, may be tamer and more on the defensive, whereas the wolf may be wild and aggressive. Check that you are telling yourself the truth on this one.

Look out for any internal conflicts, paying particular attention to any sense of unease that might indicate a lurking conflict which hasn't fully emerged. Try to tease it out, encouraging 'the wolf' and 'the dog' to declare themselves. If a complex web of factors appears, try to crystallise this into just two opposing forces.

We'll take this exercise a stage further in Chapter 5, but for now just concentrate on identifying the conflicts clearly. Sometimes just the act of observing the conflict will cause it to disappear. In any case, clarity often helps to show how the issue can be resolved.

Exercise 5: Acting Out a Conflict Ritual

Try to take part in one of the following: a martial arts session, a debate, or a dance session which involves set movements. Experience the advances and retreats, discover how potential aggression is formalised and transformed. What kind of energies arise from this? Do you gain or lose energy from it?

Exercise 6: Dance Away Your Troubles – Fantasy Conflict

Choose one current conflict that you have identified, and try turning it into a dance. Who are the opposing dancers? What do they wear? How do they look? What kind of steps can you devise for their dance? When you have visualised this, dance it out. Dance out each side in turn. If you are working in a group, split into pairs and ask your partner to represent one of the adversaries.

Another option is to turn the conflict into a fantasy as a cartoon type of battle. Allow your imagination free play, either as a visualisation, or through setting it down on paper as a drawing or a story.

Exercise 7: Making Magic Stones

This exercise is a chance to practise a little simple magic. Whatever other exercises in this chapter you leave out, don't skip this one.

The 'twin stones' referred to in the image of the dog and the wolf can also signify the twin poles of conflict. They can be a very useful device for clarifying a conflict, and for taking action if needs be.

Make two small cubes – an approximation of a cube is fine, as long as they are both the same size and shape. They should be small enough to fit easily into the palm of your hand, and light enough to carry in your pocket. You could use wood, clay (either to be fired, or the self-hardening variety) or anything else robust enough to be handled. Colour them in two strongly contrasting colours: I recommend black and white, or red and green. Decide which stone will stand for 'Yes' (positive, affirming, active), and which for 'No' (refusal, withdrawal, passive).

You can now use these to focus and implement your decisions. Start by selecting a problem or a conflict; it might be best to choose one that is not too important to begin with. Think over the problem in your mind, and turn the stones over in your hand as you do so. Focus on the problem as two polar opposites, as suggested in Exercise 4, and then consider what you want to do about it. If you want to take action, pick out the 'Yes' stone. If you are going to withdraw from the conflict, pick the 'No' stone. Hold your chosen stone for a few minutes as you affirm your decision. To help you implement this, and remind you of your purpose, you can carry the appropriate stone with you until your chosen decision is realised.

You can use different aspects of the Yes/No meanings too. For instance, 'Yes' could mean 'I'll go with the other person's decision and use the stone to help me affirm this constructively.' And 'No' could mean 'I've thought this over, and I still believe that I'm right in complaining, and I'll take the stone with me to strengthen my resolve and do it clearly.' Just be clear in your own mind how you are interpreting yes and no.

When you have finished using one of the single stones, always return it to its partner, and spend a few minutes handling them both together to restore the equilibrium.

Please do not use these stones for divination, in other words by picking one blind like tossing a coin to decide the outcome. The aim is to concentrate your own powers of gaining insight and to focus the strength of your decision-making.

The Sun needs the Moon, as the cock needs the hen.

Chapter Five

The Eternal Dynamic

I lent a book on alchemy to a friend. 'Oh, it's so *sexy*!' she enthused, when she returned it. It's true; alchemy is full of sex. Time and time again, alchemical images portray the electrifying power of sexual attraction, and the bliss as male and female unite. But the images are not just there to arouse, because sexual polarity is a Cosmic principle that operates deep within nature as well as in individual lives. Sexual energy generates the desire that helps to keep the world turning. It is also an agent of transformation, which can lead you to the roots of your being, and elevate you to the level of angels. In this chapter, we'll look at how we can classify the different types of sexual energy and experience, so that we can learn to work with them and experience some of the profounder aspects of sexuality. We'll also look at the different kinds of alchemical 'gold' created by sexual activity, and at the part played by the Worm, the Sea Serpent, the Dragon and the Angel.

The epigram for the illustration opposite reads:

O Sun, you do not act alone; without
My powers, you're a cock without a hen.
And I, the Moon, in turn require your help,
Just as the hen desires the rooster, too.
Foolish is he who wants to break apart
Those things which are conjoined in Nature's bonds.

The attraction of opposites helps the dance of life to continue. The energies of the golden sun and silver moon must combine to complete the alchemical transmutation. As the alchemist's most revered text, *The Emerald Tablet*, says: 'The father thereof is the Sun, the mother the Moon.'

To be sure, at one level the alchemists' images are a picturesque way of describing the chemical reactions in the alchemical vessel. But to practise alchemy is to explore life; the transformation takes place internally as well as in the laboratory. The alchemist must encounter his or her sexuality along the way. Even celibate alchemists, such as monks (who were some of the most notable practitioners of alchemy in the Middle Ages), would still have to channel their own sexuality into the process. In alchemy, you cannot isolate yourself from the science that you practise. The same upheavals and resolutions that occur in the laboratory will be the storms and sunshine within the alchemist's soul.

But now let's go step by step through these four different worlds, and see how they relate to sexuality. They are also allied to the four elements of earth, water, fire and air, which play a crucial part in alchemy. These elements are firmly embedded not only in the framework of alchemy, but also in other Western traditions, such as astrology, Kabbalah and ritual magic, and they signify four ascending levels of being, as well as the physical elements. Table 1 gives both their general meaning, and their interpretation within the context of alchemy.

Each of these worlds, from the most earthy to the most refined, not only has its own kind of sexual energy, but can create its own kind of

Table 1. The Four Worlds of Alchemy

Mythical Creature	Element	General Meaning	Type of Energy	Transformation into Gold	Characteristics
Worm	Earth	Instinct; physicality	Structure; form	Orgasm; conception	Physical desire
Sea Serpent	Water	Feelings; personality	Flow	Birth of love; relationship	Fantasy
Dragon	Fire	Energy; creativity	Rhythm	Power	Passion
Angel	Air	Intellect; abstract mind	Field	Knowledge	Love

gold. In alchemy, there has never been just one kind of gold – *common gold* – as the alchemists disdainfully call it, but different grades and potencies of gold, the most precious of which is known as the Elixir, because it has the power to create more gold. When it touches base matter, it transforms it to pure gold.

First World – The Kingdom of Earth

This is the world of the Worm, the level of physical response and the stirrings of sexual desire. The Worm relates to the physical organs of sex, with the 'worm' of the penis entering the accommodating 'worm-hole' of the vagina (which is in itself a kind of hollow worm shape). It represents the world of *form*, where the basic physical structures of male and female meet and mate, becoming one conjoined entity.

We've already spent some time with the Worm, but there is more to look at in terms of sexual activity. The Worm of desire flickers with interest in a potential sexual partner. And that means *any* potential partner, irrespective of age or marital status! The Worm has its own criteria. As you walk down the street, you may only half register the person coming towards you, but nevertheless, the Worm has noticed, and maybe there is a little wriggle in his or her direction. One day, walking home, I briefly caught the eye of a man coming past me and I felt that wriggle of the Worm and also captured the glimmer of a thought: 'Yes – he would do.' This struck me as strange, since at that time I wasn't in the market for a new partner. When I dug down, I found out that it was real survival stuff. As I teased out the thought, it was this: 'If I was cast away on a desert island with this man, yes, I would sleep with him. If he was the last man in the world, he would do.'

The Worm's function is to recognise attraction and repulsion, which it does despite any social norms. It serves nature and the species, as well as you as an individual. I have heard that wife-swapping parties began long before the permissive sixties. They started towards the end of the war in Germany, when the whole population was under threat. It seems that the Worm got busy stimulating lots of sexual activity in order to breed more children, and increase the mix of the gene pool.

As this is the world of physical acts and results, the gold generated in the Worm world is found in orgasm. Orgasm takes us into an explosion of feeling quite different from the pleasurable sensations that precede it during the act of sex. It is the release and transformation of energy into quite a different state. Sexual orgasm brings not only physical ecstasy, but also acts as a 'psychic clearout', ridding us of tension and negative emotion. And, just as each world offers an opportunity to go through the gateway to other worlds, so the energy of the orgasm acts like a kind of rocket which shoots up towards the heights. Sexual orgasm is known as 'the poor man's meditation'. In previous times, it was also popularly referred to as 'the little death', in the sense that it can take us beyond our personal limits.

Although orgasm is the most dramatic example of the gold created at the level of the Worm, gold can also be experienced in a more general sense here as the subtle current of sexual energy that runs through us all the time. This is not always easy to notice, but certain breathing techniques or magical practices can make a person more aware of this current, which is often experienced as a kind of liquid gold passing through the central axis of the body. It can also be perceived more easily by someone who is in a more heightened state of general sexual awareness than usual, perhaps a person in the early stages of an exciting new relationship.

There is, of course, an obvious example of transformation at the physical level of sex, which is the conception of a child when sperm meets egg, and the gold of new life is generated. In alchemy, the union of the king and queen, or sun and moon, also results in the birth of a child. But this is not the end of the process; the child must die and be reborn on a higher level before transformation is complete.

Second World — The World of Water

Moving on from the Worm, we go through a kind of transitional stage, the watery world of the Sea Serpent where our desires take form in dreams and fancies. This is to a large extent a transitional world between the Worm and the Dragon. In this underwater realm, fantasy is created. In the coils of the Sea Serpent, yearnings spiral, and longings gather and disperse, as its body writhes in an ever-changing play of iridescent beauty. This is a world of *flow* where images and desires wash in and out with no perceptible beginning or end.

We all know that fantasy plays a large part in sex. When a little extra stimulation is needed to get going, fantasy plays its part. Lovers play games, dress up, and tease each other. In a new relationship, each lover has to find out what the other likes and will be a willing party to. Secret jokes, shared dreams and pet names all begin to give the relationship its very personal and private identity. But this world is fluid, and its boundaries are not clearly defined. So this is a risky business when you are trying to put the relationship on a firm footing, as one person's fantasy can turn out to be another person's nightmare.

Although the colourful underwater garden of the Sea Serpent can be a delightful place to explore, it is no place for mortals to live permanently, as folk tales of unhappy marriages to mermaids, seals and other underwater creatures testify. It's a world which adolescents dive into, when the uprush of sexual feelings is still new, and can take safe form in fantasy. I can remember spending hours dreaming about my latest pop star idol, creating romantic scenarios in which he at last recognised our true love. However, floating in those waters for too long can be very draining of energy, and in extreme cases can even blur the edges of reality. But a refreshing dip now and again in the waters of fantasy is a natural human pleasure.

When a real relationship begins, as opposed to a fantasy one, feelings are often especially intense, and they can swirl around like great tangles of drifting seaweed, keeping us afloat when a casual word or action from the other gives cause for hope, and pulling us down to the depths when disappointment is threatened. It's hard to keep a sense of proportion in the world of water.

The Serpent's ocean world acts as the medium that connects our emotions to our physical drives. In itself, it has little substance, yet it is very powerful. It is also very important because it's here that a relationship begins to develop, as opposed to disjointed sexual encounters. What awaits us here is the genuine joy generated by sexual contact, rather than just sexual gratification, and the wonderful emotions that lovers share. The water is the birthplace of love, just as Venus was born from the waves. Like the alchemical child, though, that love has to do some growing and suffering in the worlds beyond water before it reaches its full flowering.

In certain myths, the Sea Serpent is the guardian of a wonderful pearl. This precious gem lies at the bottom of the ocean, its lustrous surface reflecting the iridescent gleam of a million dreams. As I mentioned before, pearl and gold are closely related in alchemy, so the pearl here represents the gold of the watery world. The pearl itself is a product of transformation, the grain of sand that turns into a gleaming gem within a shell that is similar to the sealed vessel of alchemy. In the world of the Sea Serpent we swim with the currents of desire, searching for that precious pearl, following the romantic dream whose treasure we believe lies somewhere deep in that ocean.

But what is the real alchemical gold to be found there? All gold in alchemy is the result of transformation. It's not there simply for the asking. It usually means sacrificing one thing to gain another, and engaging yourself fully with that process. Although feelings and imagination may be the nourishing food of this world, they have to be distilled to make gold. This means moving beyond personal responses in a relationship to a place where you can also embrace your partner's feelings and viewpoint. It can mean letting go of your own strong feelings to sense the other person's needs and desires. When you do this, something else comes in. If this is done willingly, it does not become submission to your partner's emotions, but instead helps to create the 'emotional body' of your relationship. That has a real substance of its own, even though it is delicate and changeable.

The gold of this world is not fixed, just as the world of water is forever flowing and changing. We can think of it as golden showers, or the scintillating play of light on water. If we take the alternative image of a pearl, its colours change in the light, and its lustre becomes dimmed or brightened according to its environment.

Third World — The Realm of Fire

This is the world of the Dragon, which for much of the time lies curled up in its lair. Its fire only bursts forth when it is fully roused. Then the Dragon awakes and seizes its victim, snorting flames and smoke as it flies up high into the sky. With the beat of its wings, the flight of passion has begun.

A Dragon is a kind of Worm or Serpent with wings. The Worm simply has the urge to mate, but as the Dragon's wings unfold, passion takes over. Very few sexual relationships begin with passion. They begin with the wriggle of the Worm, and are launched with the colourful dreams of the Sea Serpent. But it's usually later that the Dragon takes flight. Suddenly, the partners can hardly bear to be apart from each other, and their relationship takes precedence over everything else. More dangerously, they may have the belief that they are invulnerable. All Dragons believe that they cannot be conquered, but we know from myths and legends that they can be defeated by the sword, often because of their great pride.

A Dragon of passion can exist in other forms apart from sexuality, such as the grip of religious fervour, or fierce devotion to a cause. It is the nature of Dragons to take hold, and though we may feel that we are the ones who are soaring effortlessly, it maybe that the Dragon's claws grip us tightly and we cannot escape. But when the end does come, it is usually a painful business, and may mean being dropped from a great height.

Lovers always believe that they are unique, and that their passion will last forever. We smile indulgently when we hear this. Or maybe it irritates us – how can they possibly believe that they are the only ones to feel like this? But it is deadly serious when you yourself are tumbled into the storm of passion. Plenty of people imagine that they are invulnerable until it happens to them, often at the most inappropriate time. Everything feels different when you are flying with the Dragon. All of life is more colourful and exciting, so the fired-up lover tackles even the most mundane tasks with enthusiasm. Extraordinary levels of energy and a rush of creative vision flood in. You can sometimes spot Dragon energy at work, even when the person is trying to conceal it. I met a friend of mine one evening, and thought that she was looking unnaturally, feverishly bright. She was even wearing orange, the colour of Dragon fire. What I didn't know at the time was that she was having a secret and illicit affair. Shortly afterwards, she left her home and her children to go with her lover, and a lot of suffering followed that decision.

But maybe it's better to know the Dragon than to run scared from it all your life. Many of us have embarked on crazy adventures, or have had reckless affairs that have collapsed in spectacular fashion. Should we not have gone down that route? I doubt it. By encountering that energy, we begin to recognise it and that knowledge will give us choice in the future. People don't usually have more than two or three full-blown 'Dragon episodes' in their lives. And even an episode that ends painfully can have its value. It can transform a person's emotions and outlook, and set them on a new path, although it may leave cruel wounds. It *is* possible to conquer the Dragon, and you can't do that without taking risks. When conquered, you will have energy, creativity and charisma at your disposal, though you will always need to use it wisely; you can never trust a Dragon, not for one moment.

Dragon gold is red gold. This gold is smelted and forged, and wondrous shapes can be beaten from it. This is the world of fire, and also of *rhythm*, just as the hammer beats out the gold and the Dragon's leathery wings beat in its flight through the sky. The rhythm of the sexual act is mirrored in the mounting of passion. Rhythm generates excitement, and some people deliberately play a love affair hot and cold in turn to intensify the level of excitement. This Dragon world is one where the physical and emotional desires of the lovers synchronise; their pulses begin to beat as one. As they synchronise, so passion escalates. Then the lovers can rise above the physical level, and forge the gold of creative energy. Lovers can indeed achieve miracles, inspiring one another, implementing major life changes together, or working together as partners in business, art or performance. Just as a beautifully wrought golden brooch may last for thousands of years, so a tale of passionate love becomes a myth that endures in the telling, such as the stories of Tristan and Iseult, Eloise and Abelard, and Romeo and

Juliet. Although these lovers are often ill-fated, their passion triumphs and death and misfortune cannot wipe out the enduring power of their relationship. There are songs which tell of roses growing out of the lovers' graves, and intertwining as they blossom, triumphant over death and the evil of their enemies.

Fourth World – The Field of Air

From the Dragon, we move into the world of the Angel. An Angel generates a kind of radiant field which is above the storm of the Dragon's wing-beats, and untroubled by the slithering of the Worm. As you enter the world of Angels, you are transported into another realm. The heady excitement of the Dragon world dissolves, and instead you may experience calm, peace of mind and the sense that all is well. It's a glimpse that we may only occasionally attain, but just one 'angelic moment' can sustain us for a long time to come.

> *Once or twice, in the car when driving home,*
> *Or perhaps at a pause in our conversation,*
> *We entered the realm of the angels.*
> *There was a steadiness, like a room always lit,*
> *where all is reconciled*
> *and questions no longer need be asked.*
> *I could live contented in that room*
> *where we enter the timeless zone,*
> *and absences and meetings have no meaning.*
> (from a poem by the author)

Angels have hit the headlines in recent years, after suffering years of neglect. So I would like to take a little time here to explore what we mean by Angels and the angelic, before putting this into the context of sexuality and relationships.

The appearance of an Angel is a sign of a higher world breaking through into our human world. Our normal patterns of action and reaction are suspended when this happens; mysterious or miraculous events may occur as a result of the Angel's presence. Most people who have witnessed the appearance of an Angel (and this seems to be a common experience) are given hope by the encounter. Angels bring testimony that there is more to our universe than meets the eye, and they bring us the assurance that, sometimes at least, we may be watched over, helped and protected.

Angels, or winged beings, are acknowledged in cultures throughout the world, so it is safe to say that they represent a real level of human experience. But the description of them varies, suggesting that we interpret their presence in our own way. There is a range of ways in which people experience Angels. An Angel may be seen as a winged figure, heard as a voice, or even felt as softly beating wings. Sometimes people claim to have met an Angel in the guise of an ordinary human being. Some cultures believe that a stranger asking for hospitality may be an Angel, and so the unexpected guest must always be well treated.

The word Angel comes from the Greek *angelos*, and means 'messenger'. In the Christian tradition, which grew out of Assyrian and Jewish mythology, they are seen as messengers operating between God and mankind, as well as playing an important role in sustaining the whole of Creation. In general, we can say that Angels mediate between higher and lower worlds. In terms of individual encounters with Angels, we can perhaps understand this better if we describe the experience as an 'angelic moment', something which may have the qualities of Angels being present, but without necessarily getting a visual or sensory impression of them. This can be an awesome experience, one which does not fit into the normal framework of time and space. For some people this feels like returning home, whereas for others it can be quite frankly terrifying. We touch on a world where the impossible becomes possible.

The most appropriate way to consider Angels here is by exploring the *angelic level* of sex and relationships. The *angelic moment* comes when a lover enters this realm. Such a moment may happen after making love, when the Worm of desire and the Dragon of passion are spent. Normal boundaries dissolve; you may feel that you are physically in a place which is more spacious, and both lighter and brighter than usual. This is not just the result of the pleasant afterglow from sex.

It is a real transformation of your state. A common feeling at this time is that your union is greater than the sum of the two of you as individuals. Your personal boundaries are no longer tightly drawn, yet you do not feel threatened by their dissolution. Disagreements fall away. Anxieties and insecurities disappear. You accept that what exists, exists. What will be, will be. Love and trust are present.

> *They're lovers again: Sugar dissolving in milk.*
> *Day and night, no difference. The sun is the moon:*
> *An amalgam. Their gold and silver melt together…*
> *Men and angels speak one language.*
> *The elusive ones finally meet.*
> (from a poem by Rumi)

This is the world of *air* and of *field*, as in a field of energy. From this union of two lovers a field of consciousness has come into being, a space filled with golden light. Thoughts, feelings, bodies all sink to their proper level. Even the Dragon's wing-beats slow down as his fire is used up, and he returns to his lair, leaving the pure air to the creatures of spirit.

There is an old saying, that when a silence suddenly falls in the conversation, an Angel is passing overhead. This is not only a beautiful belief, but it may have a grain of truth in it. When the everyday hubbub stills, we have a chance of entering the angelic realm. Trivial concerns melt away, and we can find ourselves listening – maybe to music we can only faintly hear. At this time there may be a sense of communion between those present. And then people look at each other, laugh and the spell is broken. It dissolves as fast as it came.

There is a chance to sustain this, though, especially between lovers who are already in strong communion, and who may be in a state of heightened consciousness in each other's presence. In that moment, you may find that you *know*. What do you know? Perhaps something about the forces of life that brought the two of you together, and the path that you are on. Perhaps you will have a glimpse into the future. For some, it may be a religious experience. Sexuality has long been seen as the gateway to higher knowledge.

As you look into the eyes of your lover, you may see the presence of an Angel. You are looking beyond the personality, beyond desire into his or her essential nature. This is the most unguarded moment of all, and usually only a pair of lovers or a mother and child have the trust to gaze into each other's eyes without any pretence.

These angelic moments touch upon our common humanity, because beyond the field of gold generated by two lovers there is an even greater field of common life in which we all participate. Here reside knowledge and love. Love has transcended selfish desires; it includes all life.

But the Sea Serpent is waiting to pull us down quick as lightning into the waters of fancy. Sentimentality and fear can close the doors to the angelic realm. To be fair, it is almost impossible to sustain that connection for very long. When faced with the unfamiliar we try to interpret the experience and in doing so, we lose it. We may try to analyse what's going on, and suddenly it's not happening any more. Or we sense the power of this moment and run scared from it. There is also the danger of attributing grandiose notions to it ('Ah – now I know! We were priest and priestess together in Ancient Egypt!'). No, you are priest and priestess *now* – or you were, until this tempting thought entered your mind.

Sexual energy can transform from its roots in desire, through the watery world of dreams to the burning energy of Dragon excitement, and finally find a safe haven in the clear, calm world of the angelic. Even the Dragon is still confined in time and space, but the Angel can transcend that. Any intention, wish or prayer that is raised to the level of the Angel can have extraordinary results.

The ideas and work I suggest here are intended to help us understand our sexual relationships better, and also to open up possibilities for transformation within them. Observing sexual energy helps us to separate out the different levels of our experience, to see how it moves between the worlds of physical desire, emotions, passionate energy and transcendent joy.

Work For This Chapter

I have set out the work for this chapter in a slightly different form. These are not so much exercises, but more suggestions for finding the power and the wonder that is within your own sexual experience. You may find them relevant to practise now, or prefer to wait for a more appropriate time. They can in theory be done by adults of any age. They are not intended to disrupt relationships or cause trouble in anybody's life. However, proceed carefully, lightly, and with consideration for others.

Making Gold in the World of the Worm

Watch the arising of desire. Try to catch it unawares, even when you are walking down the street. Be ready to acknowledge it, even if you would rather ignore it. For example, if you are a lady of 60-plus who feels a tickle of desire when an 18-year-old male comes into view, that's fine. You don't have to act on it. At least, not fully. But when you catch the upsurge of desire, see if you can use it, not to get into a specifically sexual situation, but as a type of energy which can enliven the interaction and maybe brighten up someone else's day. It is still sexual energy, and works by polarising with the other person; everyone has their own style, but it is often channelled through paying focused and courteous attention to the other person. It sometimes involves joking, implied admiration and even an unashamed dash of flirtation. As one person projects a little bit of energy, the other catches it, and sends back the energy with something of their own added to it. This means that the energy increases and brightens, but is kept light and within bounds. The chances are that you are quite familiar with this technique already, but have never watched it properly in action. As with anything you choose to operate consciously, you can hone the intention so that it works more cleanly, develop your skill, and handle the interaction with a lighter touch, letting it go gracefully when the moment is right to do so.

Making Gold in the World of the Sea Serpent

Under the ocean, the Sea Serpent lives in a jewelled palace with a beautiful garden. He guards a pearl which you must take from him and give to your lover. Create your own version of this story by writing it, retelling it or using it as a visualisation. What happens in the palace? What is the pearl like? Who is your lover – and what does the gift of the pearl signify?

In real life, give a gift to your lover. It may be material, sexual or from the heart. Choose it carefully; give it willingly, without demands or strings attached.

Making Gold in the World of the Dragon

Observe your own rhythms of sexual desire, and your cycles of passion or enthusiasm. If you are in a relationship, and want to increase its energy and your mutual desire, try synchronising your rhythms of desire with those of your partner, so that both pulses of energy beat together. If you want to slow things down, then adjust your rhythm so that it acts as a cross-beat to your partner's, to calm and soothe. Do not cut off from the other person (which is hurtful and provocative) but keep your own pulse of response steady.

Learning to ride the Dragon is the challenge of this level. Doing this transforms the Dragon's fire from destructive flame to golden energy.

Making Gold in the World of the Angel

Look out for those moments that I have described, when communion between people enters another realm. Look out especially for those silences which can fall suddenly in the middle of conversation or interaction. Is there a heightened energy, a presence which you can commune with at that time? By tuning into it yourself, you are likely to draw your partner into it too. If you do not have a partner, or a relationship suitable for this, you can find such moments with other companions. When they arise, do not rush to interpret them. Treat this as a new world that you can explore.

Gold here is light, a golden radiance which suffuses you and the space you find yourself in.

This lion has no feathers; the other has.

Chapter Six

* * * * * * * * * * * * * * *

Flying High

This brings us to one of the most curious stages in alchemy, which happens after the marriage of the King and Queen, and the birth of their child. You might think that the story should end happily there. But now this child has to die. Why should this be?

At this stage, the mystical element comes into our alchemical journey. Up till now, we've been dealing mainly with personal dynamics. Now comes the point when we must transcend those. The personalities of the alchemical King and Queen become irrelevant. Even their beautiful child, product of a blissful marriage, must die to be born again in a higher form.

Alchemy is a very slippery subject. No two writers describe it in exactly the same way. There is no set number of stages in the process, though there are plenty of similar images and descriptions to be found in the alchemical literature. But one stage that practically all the sources are agreed on is that of 'putrefaction': a death followed by a resurrection. At the point where the alchemical death takes place, everything seems lost. But then the miracle of new life appears.

And of true Putrefying, remember this,
For then to alter perfectly thou may not miss;
And thus by the Gate of Blackness thou must come in
To light of Paradise in Whiteness if thou wilt win.
(The Compound of Alchemy – George Ripley*)*

In alchemy, you often have to look behind the scenes to find out what is really going on. Death, whether it is symbolic or literal, means that the bonds of body and spirit are loosed, and thus the individual identity dissolves. So one of the important questions to ask here is: What happens when those bonds are loosed? Can alchemy tell us not only about the death and rebirth process itself, but about the potential that is released during that process? We don't have to go far into the alchemical accounts to find clues. The emblem chosen for this chapter from *Atlanta Fugiens* shows us the way:

> *The LION, king of beasts and strong of heart*
> *And claws, fights fearless and disdains to flee.*
> *You join to him the winged Lioness:*
> *She tries to fly up, carrying the male.*
> *But he will hold his ground, and keep her down;*
> *May nature's image show to you the way.*

The winged lioness, like an ancient sky goddess, flies upwards. The spirit ascends, and tries to draw the body with it. But the body is too heavy, and the old bonds that kept the lioness and her mate together have weakened. Nevertheless, the earthly lion body also struggles to keep his spirit mate with him. The pair need to separate before they can be transformed, and reunited in a new form. In other alchemical texts this process is sometimes illustrated as two birds in the nest, one trying to fly away, and the other holding it back.

All this gets quite complicated if we take the other image into account, that of the alchemical child who has been born and now must die. In alchemy, when in doubt, remember the principle of a pair of opposites united by a third ingredient, the three together forming a harmonious and integrated whole. What gives the process its dynamic though, is that this 'whole' must be constantly broken down and re-formed at a higher level. So the union of King and Queen was first of all cemented by the birth of a child. Now the child, the third force, and the soul of the marriage, dies, thus loosening the ties between King and Queen, and leaving them in the wilderness. Then the child will come to life again in a higher form, and his growth will set the King and Queen back on their throne.

What we will look at in this chapter is the nature of that 'wilderness', and the re-entry into a higher form of life.

The View from the Mountain

Some alchemical writings make it clear that this time of flight is a chance to know the country of the spirit. One of the most profoundly mystical of alchemical texts, *The Book of Lambspring*, shows this as two figures standing on the summit of a high mountain. A winged Guide has led the royal son of the alchemical marriage to the heights, and now offers to show him wonderful sights:

> *The Guide addresses the Son in these words:*
> *Come hither! I will conduct thee everywhere,*
> *To the summit of the loftiest mountain,*
> *That thou mayest understand all wisdom,*
> *That thou mayest behold the greatness of the earth, and of the sea,*
> *And thence derive true pleasure.*
> *I will bear thee through the air*
> *To the gates of highest heaven.*
> *The Son hearkened to the words of the Guide,*
> *And ascended upward with him;*
> *There he saw the heavenly throne,*
> *That was beyond measure glorious.*

However, in the midst of this splendid vision, the son remembers his father the king whom he has abandoned below, and asks the Guide to let him return:

> *When he had beheld these things,*
> *He remembered his Father with sighing,*
> *Pitied the great sorrow of his Father,*
> *And said: I will return to his breast*
> *I will go down to my Father,*
> *For he cannot live without me.*
> *He sighs and calls aloud for me.*

When the son returns, his father literally gobbles him up with joy, swallowing him whole. Then, the King, lying on his bed in a fever after such a rash move, prays to God to restore his son to life. A silver rain descends from the stars, softening the King's body, turning it into limpid water. From this sacred water, both the King and his son are born anew. They have passed through the darkness:

> *Thus in divers things*
> *They produce untold, precious fruit.*
> *They perish never more,*
> *And laugh at death.*

The Guide becomes their permanent companion.

> *Upon one throne they sit,*
> *And the face of the Ancient Master*
> *Is straightway seen between them:*
> *He is arrayed in a crimson robe.*
> *(The Book of Lambspring – Anon)*

I've quoted at length from this remarkable book because it has resonance on so many different levels. Its powerful images and effortless poetry illuminate different types of situations, from the physical changes in the alchemical vessel to the mysteries of the spirit. Some of the images have had great significance for me personally over the years. When doing astrological or divination readings for others, I have always held image of the Guide showing the view from the top of the mountain as my own ideal. Nowadays many astrologers regard their work as healing or therapy, but for myself I have always seen it as the way of the Guide, leading someone to the highest point so that they can see the landscape, and the lay-out of the country that they inhabit. From this they will quite literally gain new perspectives, and from these new choices may unfold.

The sorrows of the father left below can be seen as the symptoms of a body left almost uninhabited while the spirit wanders off to view the higher realms; we can look at this a little later on in terms of psychic activity. But this passage also strikes such a note of compassion, as essential humanity responds to the ties of love, that it brings a moral dimension into the picture. It is not enough to roam the halls of heaven and gain wondrous knowledge; we must bring all this back to base, and use it to help ease suffering and lighten the daily struggle.

In this example, the real death point comes as the son tries to return to his father, and the situation that he left behind. But this is not to be; there is no going back. The son is eaten by his father, and both must now die to give way to new life. A sacrifice is made. Later in this book, we will be looking at the idea of giving service when we have gained knowledge, and this often means putting aside personal ambitions, something that this alchemical death may symbolise.

Finally, in looking at the symbolism of this story, we mustn't forget the Guide. Who is he? Once again, alchemy plays with different ideas at once. He is certainly the winged and wise Hermes Trismegistus, the patron of alchemy. In this particular account, he may also stand for the Holy Ghost of the Christian Trinity, because the anonymous author has chosen to represent a male triad, as opposed to the more usual one found in alchemy of King, Queen and royal son. But the Guide also represents the soul of the seeker. Once body, soul and spirit have been restored to life, and are aligned in a new and permanent harmony, even greater miracles are possible.

An earlier emblem in *The Book of Lambspring* explains this further, illustrating a unicorn and a deer deep in a forest.

> *We shall call the forest the Body…*
> *The unicorn will be the Spirit at all times.*
> *The deer desires no other name*
> *But that of the Soul…*
> *He that knows how to tame and master them by Art,*
> *To couple them together,*
> *And to lead them in and out of the forest,*
> *May justly be called a Master.*

This is an astounding suggestion, that we may gain the power to 'lead' the soul and spirit in and out of the body at will. The implication is that the soul and spirit, permanently confined to the 'forest' of the body, cannot develop their true capabilities. But complete freedom from the body cannot be sustained in this life. So the alchemist should develop the skill of leading soul and spirit in and out of the dark forest. This is advanced work of a true master alchemist.

Let's move on to looking at these questions in terms of everyday life. I'm hoping that alchemy will do double duty here in helping to explain both the kind of events that can occur during the course of our lives, and also the process that unfolds when we actively pursue the path of transformation. Although you cannot make a hard and fast distinction between the two, there is a difference between events which crop up of their own accord, and the experiences which result from active alchemical work.

If you follow the path of transformation, then at some point you will hit this point of 'mortification' and 'putrefaction', as the alchemists described it. You must pass through the gate into the darkness of the unknown. This stage is also known as 'The Raven's Wing' and it may occur just after an especially fruitful period, which is called 'The Peacock's Tail'. However much we prepare for this moment, we never really believe that we will hit such a reversal of fortune. In the early stages of the work we are often more self-assured than later on. When you set out on a spiritual path you quickly gain confidence in the tradition you are following. Often the best instructors (rather than teachers) are found among students with only three or four years' experience. They are clear-headed, enthusiastic, secure in their knowledge and keen to get others working along the right lines too.

To begin with, it all appears to be quite straightforward. But later on comes the time of darkness when all this confidence falls away. When I began meditation practice at the age of 19, I was convinced that I would be enlightened by the time I was 24. It seems a ridiculous idea now, and I'm rather ashamed to admit it! If I try and tap into that memory now, I find that it was not so much a conviction of impending enlightenment as a sense that this work would sort my life out, and abolish my doubts and fears. Then I would have nothing more to worry about, and everything would be plain sailing. It would give me, in other words, a quick-fix solution to life's problems. Some 30-odd years later, I now know that no kind of spiritual training can guarantee you an easy passage through life. Nothing in this life is in a permanent state; when change stops, life stops. And as changes continue, they throw up new challenges. The training that you receive helps you to deal with them, not delete them. Enlightenment, like the alchemist's finest gold, means gaining a foothold in the eternal world, not absolute mastery over the woes of this world. As the alchemists say: 'Our gold is not common gold.'

The moment when alchemical darkness and death arrives is of a major order. It may happen several times over in our lives; although the alchemical process can be laid out rather neatly from beginning to end, in fact we move through different cycles, and different phases of development occur on different levels. So the process can be repeated over and over again in different ways.

I remember being on a course one summer when the first such recognisable 'death' came. I woke up in the middle of the night in anguish; I felt utterly alone and without hope. This world had receded, but there was nothing to take its place. The following day I could do nothing but cry. This was no ordinary emotional upset, but something that had disturbed the roots of my being.

My teacher took me out for a walk. 'This moment,' he said gently, 'we call the birth of the soul. All births are painful.'

I looked at him, amazed. It didn't feel like anything except pain. But, in fact, it was a point of major change for me. My earlier confidence had been destroyed at one blow, but something new was pushing upwards, like shoots forcing their way through the soil.

The idea that the soul should be 'born' may at first strike you as a strange one. The Hermetic tradition says that each person is born with the basic capacity to have a soul, but it tends to remain innate, and unorganised. Spiritual work or life experience can bring it fully into being. Once 'born', it is like an organ; it is a faculty through which we can sense the nature of other souls around us. It is a mediator between higher and lower worlds, and is sometimes seen as a chalice into which the spirit can be poured.

Other experiences of 'mortification' may include tragic life events, which can tear apart the calm confidence of the spiritually well-trained person. A death in the family, betrayal by a partner, the collapse of a professional career – these are just some of the obvious events which can trigger the moment of darkness. We learn that however serious our dedication to spiritual development, it cannot protect us from external blows. A person who has been through such traumas, however, will find that his or her training helps to integrate them. It is also possible to see them as part of the process of transformation and growth and he or she may emerge stronger as a result.

On the alchemical path, we must accept what is happening, and have faith that we will move through it. Although we may pass through the gate into the unknown, our spirit has a chance to soar; we can fly like the winged lion, and climb up the mountain with the Guide. The Guide is always there to be found, whether you acknowledge him as your Guardian Angel, your Higher Self, or wise Hermes Trismegistus. From that mountaintop we may see wonders, even though we are still suffering like the King left bereft below.

Work For This Section

If you have suffered such a time already, cast your mind back and ask whether you also experienced something of a higher order. Did you gain spiritual knowledge? Did you notice such a separation from your old self, where perhaps you went through great pain of one kind or another yet you were also able to receive new understanding or illumination?

Into the Unknown

Every disaster, tragedy, or setback can be material for new life when rebirth comes. A person who has moved through such a dark period usually develops compassion and deeper understanding of life. No one can really teach others until they have passed through this point – they can only 'instruct' as I suggested earlier.

Some traditions actually engineer a symbolic death experience to stimulate this leap into the unknown. Shamanic traditions are particularly noted for this, and the candidate for initiation may be sealed up in a 'vision pit' for days, deprived of food, water and company. He must 'die' to himself; he (or she) may pass through agonies of physical pain, and mental anguish. Then, when all normality is swept away, the vision may come. In shamanism, this can be the appearance of a spirit in the form of a bird or animal; this represents the guide and guardian of the shaman, who will become a source of help for the shaman's healing work in the community. However, this comes at a price; shamans usually have to relinquish any claim on a personal life. They may be required to live alone, giving up their personal contact with friends and family, and their society may fear them as much as respect them. Their mission becomes their life.

Vigils and rituals involving isolation in darkness are found in Western religious and magical traditions too, though they are not usually carried out to such an extreme extent. The candidate for knighthood used to spend the night alone in a dark chapel before receiving his initiation the following day. Such a process would help the him to strip away all the normal trappings of daily life, and be thrown back on his own resources. It is at the point of complete isolation or 'alone-ness' that a breakthrough into another world can take place. You must experience your aloneness before you discover that the world doesn't end there, at your personal limits. Of course, a three-hour solitary vigil is not going to achieve total transformation every time. But bear in mind that a ritual is also a way of preparing you to meet these challenges on a bigger scale. If you have endured even a few hours of darkness and deprivation, symbolic or literal, you are going to be much better equipped to face the same kind of experience in the future. We are creatures who instinctively understand symbolic action and its link to events in 'real time'. Sometimes people think that a ritual which does not cause an immediate and dramatic change is useless, but it is not. It is training for body and mind.

There is a very real chance of a breakthrough into a world beyond normal personal limitations. One night, I lay in bed in the dark, wide-awake because I was going through some emotional distress. I could not rid myself of these feelings, so I decided to let the pain intensify rather than to try and ease it. It grew stronger but more focussed, centring on the solar plexus area. It built towards an agonising climax, then suddenly, it disappeared entirely, and I found myself in a completely different world. Words are inadequate to describe the nature of this shift and the new realm that I discovered. I was in a different state of consciousness altogether, freer and larger. I found that I could 'move' in any direction I wanted. I could ask questions, and know the answers. This was a multi-dimensional 'place' where knowledge abounded, and my own personal limitations were stripped away. I asked questions about various people I knew, and in the same moment I received knowledge about them. Their potential and character were revealed to me with startling clarity. I would have been happy to stay there practically forever, but after half an hour or so the world returned to normal.

Often, the test of such experiences is in the quality they leave behind. In this instance, my earlier emotional distress had completely dissolved, and the experience that had caused it now seemed rather unimportant. It was still the middle of the night, but I was full of energy. I had to get up, and go and make myself something to eat. I couldn't go back to bed, and I faced the next day refreshed and full of vigour. The insights that I gained that night remained, and even to this day, about ten years later, they continue to shed light on the people and situations that I queried at that time.

So far, so good. But there is one danger with this type of experience, and that is the desire to repeat it. I am not unique; many people have 'transcendent moments', and these often occur at times of extreme physical or mental duress. Once access is gained to the supra-personal realm, it is natural to want to go back there again. And it is a great temptation to try and re-create the conditions that brought the moment about. People who were under physical stress may put themselves over and over again into similarly dangerous situations (driving fast, mountain-climbing or whatever) in the hope of breaking through the elusive barrier. For quite a long time afterwards, I was tempted to intensify any emotional pain, to use it as a kind of springboard into the other world. It has never worked again though – luckily for me, I suspect!

It is rarely necessary to try and get back into that experience. But what you can do is to keep a point of access to it – not re-live it, but just find a way of touching it again so that some kind of channel is kept open between the worlds.

This stage of alchemy throws up a great deal for us to consider, more than one chapter can do justice to. But we should certainly take a look though at the question of psychic activity before we move on. The idea of leading soul and spirit in and out of the body, illustrated in *The Book of Lambspring*, suggests out-of-the-body experiences. These occur unbidden to countless people, sometimes at the time of an accident or a brush with death, sometimes on the edges of sleeping and waking, and sometimes to people who just seem to have trouble staying in their body the whole time. They are not an essential part of working with alchemy, but you may experience them either because you are that way inclined, or the work that you do may stimulate them to happen. In any case, the physical type of out-of-the-body experiences (if that doesn't sound too paradoxical) are similar in some respects to those which accompany certain spiritual experiences, and even bear some relation to the practice of meditation or visualisation. The bonds between body, soul and spirit can be loosened at this time.

I had a dramatic experience of this when I was thrown from a horse and knocked unconscious for a few minutes. When I came to, I couldn't remember anything, but I realised that the face of the woman looking down at me seemed familiar. In fact it was the young woman who had been helping me to school my horse, but at first I didn't recognise her. I gazed into her face and thought, 'How lovely you are! Yes, I really love you.' I was simply full of love for a fellow human being. Somehow, everything else had been knocked out of the frame and I was experiencing the love that connects us all to each other. Although I had physical pain and shock from the accident, it was almost worth it just to discover how closely we are all bonded under the surface. When I visited a friend in hospital who was seriously ill with meningitis, something similar occurred. She didn't know who I was, but gave me a beautiful, trusting smile just as a young baby might. Later, all her mental functions returned and so the next time I saw her we had a perfectly normal conversation. She didn't remember my earlier visit at all. But I felt a new and deeper bond with her after that wonderful smile, when the normal mask of the personality was stripped away.

However, the main point of this story is something rather different. For a few hours after my accident my memory of that day was completely fragmented, and I puzzled over how the story fitted together. With difficulty, I eventually managed to remember how I was jumping the horse, then how he reared up and came down with me, and finally how he galloped back to the stable with stirrups flapping ......But wait a minute! I couldn't have seen that last part. I was unconscious at the time. And even if I hadn't been, from where I lay a stone wall would have blocked my view of the horse. So what I saw was only visible from a higher place. The memory wouldn't go away. It was a perfectly normal, unexceptional image – except that in theory I couldn't have seen it. I gradually realised that I had had an out-of-the-body experience. I had been lying unconscious on the ground, yet I *had* seen Cally the horse running away, and this had been from a point way above my body.

There are many such stories. A woman I met told me how she was involved in a serious car accident. She was profoundly unconscious, yet she remembers looking down on the scene from a great height, and seeing her dog thrown out of the car. Later, as she was lying still apparently profoundly unconscious in hospital, she heard two doctors discussing her case and saying that if she regained consciousness, she would be brain-damaged. 'Surely they can't be talking about *me?*' she thought.

We know very little in scientific terms about how these sorts of experiences happen, and how consciousness can possibly 'relocate' itself away from the normal physical framework of the senses. Yet my own and others' experiences testify that this is so. In the language of the psychics, we have a 'silver cord' which tethers us to our body if we temporarily shift outside it, and which helps us to find our way back into it. Mediums who go into a trance must be able to slip back easily into their bodies, and thus they should not be startled or woken abruptly. You may notice that some children also get very upset if they are woken up suddenly, and we are always cautioned to treat sleep-walkers gently.

Psychic experiences need not be out-of-body experiences though, and the majority probably are not. Practically everyone has them from time to time: you are about to ring a friend when she rings you, or you find yourself in a place that you have already dreamed about, but never visited in real life before. You may suddenly know what's coming in today's post, or move your valuables to the bank just before a burglary. No one can predict accurately all the time, or lotteries and betting on horse races would grind to a standstill. And if you are determined to demonstrate your powers to others, they have a funny way of disappearing altogether.

Divination practices, such as Tarot, palmistry and astrology, are linked to the intuitive and psychic faculties. They give a chance for the feathered lioness to fly, but they also have a framework and technique which tethers us to reality like the lion below. Some divination systems such as astrology have a lot of technique, whereas others, like the Tarot, rely far more on intuition. Ancient oracles, like the Oracle of Delphi, often involved some kind of ecstasy or trance for the medium, but most of the divination systems we have today, thankfully, don't require this. However, if you practise divination, you will still need to set up special conditions to do this. You might prepare a room by cleaning it, arranging the furniture, and making sure that phones, visitors etc will not interrupt you. Even if you have to make do with a table in the corner of a noisy pub (the famous seventeenth-century astrologer William Lilley conducted practically all his business in coffee houses), you can still make it a 'sacred space'. A divination always, in some sense, takes place in a sacred space, and in sacred time.

Work For This Section

Exercise 1: A Protection Ritual

Purpose: To protect a room that you wish to use for meditation or spiritual work. This may also be carried out effectively in a group. It is best to use it in a space where no one else apart from yourself or your group has legitimate reason to enter at this time, in other words, not in a public space, or you could create a conflict.

Visualise four very tall Angels made of blue light, standing one in each corner of the room. Their wings are folded. Now allow their wings to unfold and stretch out, so that the wingtip of one Angel touches the wingtip of another. Their wings together now encircle the whole space, and the room is protected.

When you have completed your work, return to your visualisation of the Angels, and ask them to fold their wings. Thank them for their protection, and release them.

Exercise 2: Entering the Unknown – A Night Vigil

Prepare a room so that it will be as dark as possible, without any light seeping through. Decide where you will sit, either on the floor or on an upright chair.

The best time to do this is in the middle of the night, at a time when you are not normally awake and it's dark outside. Go to your prepared room and sit there for one hour. (You can take an alarm clock or timer in with you, but avoid the temptation to look at it while the hour is passing). Let your usual thoughts and concerns die down as far as possible, but stay awake. If you get sleepy or cramped you can move or stretch.

After about 20 minutes or half an hour (you will have to guess this as best as you can), practise the 'Dark Cauldron' exercise. This consists of mentally discarding everything that you may consider essential to your existence.

The Dark Cauldron - In front of you stands a huge cauldron. Once anything is thrown into it, it is never seen again. Now throw away, one by one, all the things that have meaning to you – your work, your friends, your home, your clothes, your possessions, your family, and even your body. You can break these down into components – husband, best dress, legs etc. This is purely a mental exercise, and need not be accompanied by any physical gestures.

When you have discarded everything, ask yourself: 'What is left?'

Then banish the Cauldron completely, and remember this is an exercise designed to take you to your own core, not to indicate how much you value what you have discarded.

Stand up, move around the dark room a little, then sit again to complete your hour's vigil.

Afterwards, leave the room, switch on some lights, and have something to eat or drink before settling down for the rest of the night.

This exercise is also suitable for group work, and can be done with a group in a partially-darkened room at a normal meeting time, if the group leader takes the role of asking the questions.

Divination

The following are optional exercises, designed to give you a 'taster' of divination practice. If you enjoy these, and feel that they are appropriate for you, you can follow up through learning a complete system such as Tarot or astrology.

Exercise 3: Divining With a Pendulum – 'Dowsing'

Make a pendulum from a ring, a large heavy bead, or a coin with a hole in it – anything that has just enough weight to swing well at the end of a cord. Take a length of thin cord and tie the object to one end, leaving at least 20cm of cord free. Hold this cord between thumb and forefinger, with light support from the other fingers as necessary. You should hold it firmly enough so that it doesn't slip from your grasp, but not so tightly as to restrict the movement. Practice will show you how.

Begin by finding out what your responses are for 'Yes' and 'No'. Sit down, relax and hold the pendulum a little way above a surface such as a table, or the floor if you are sitting on the ground. This is the normal way to work. Let the pendulum dangle and think: 'Yes!' over and over again. What does the pendulum do? Does it swing in a straight line, or in a circle? Then repeat the exercise with: 'No!' Do this several times.

The most common response is a swing of a straight line for 'Yes' and a circling movement for 'No', but it can vary from person to person. It might even vary from day to day too, so always begin your dowsing session with this exercise. When you are confident of these responses, you are ready to start working. All dowsing is based on a simple response of the Yes/No type. Even divining for water is really a 'Yes – there is water here' kind of practice.

There are many dowsing exercises you can perform, and once you've got the hang of it, you can invent your own. The important criteria are:

- Never force the pendulum to move, nor prevent it from moving.
- Do not try and change its type of movement, however unexpected it may be.
- Keep an open mind as to the results.

● Expect it to work better at certain times than at others.

The following suggestions for dowsing range from questions about what is physically present to determining a location through map dowsing, and for insight into the past and the future.

Dowsing Objects

Get a friend to hide a few objects under cups or containers. One of them should be something of yours. Try to find where your possession is by dowsing over each of the containers in turn, asking 'Is it here?' (Yes/No).

You can also use this technique for determining which objects belong to a woman, and which to a man. First of all, check your pendulum for 'Male' and 'Female' in the same way as you tested for 'Yes' and 'No'. You can use a picture of a man and a woman to dowse over if this helps to sort out the 'code'.

Map Dowsing

There are many types of questions you can ask here. It may be better to start with one to which you can find out the answer straight away. For instance, you can ask a friend for permission to dowse where one of their relations comes from.

Use a map of the country concerned, spread it out, and divide it either by eye or by using the grid lines. Ask, 'Is it in this half?' Hopefully, your pendulum will say 'No' to one half, and 'Yes' to the other. When you have a positive response over one half, divide that into two quarters, and test each quarter. Then halve the positive quarter again, and carry on until you are left with an area too small to divide any more. This is your answer.

You can also try map dowsing for prediction, asking a question such as 'Where will I/my friend live next?' or 'Where will the next letter I receive have been posted?'

Timeline Dowsing

Draw a long line lengthways along a piece of A4 (or larger) paper.

You are going to explore this timeline in terms of where you feel most resonance or affinity. Dowse over each of the three sections – all may react positively, with your 'Yes!' code, or just one or two, or none. If you get a positive response, draw further lines in the relevant sections, dividing them up into centuries or millennia in the case of the ancient times. Test each section again, marking the ones that are resonant and positive for you. These can indicate a period of history that you have a particular affinity with, or that you have contact with a particular tradition stemming from that era. For instance, an astrologer might have a positive response to 500BC, when astrology came together as a system. Some people would even see this as indicating periods of past lives, but this should always be treated with caution.

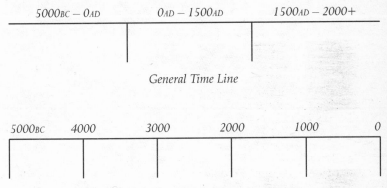

General Time Line

Example of Expanded Time Line for Response to 5000BC — 0AD

Like the Salamander, the Stone lives in the Fire.

Chapter Seven

· · · · · · · · · · · · · · · · · · ·

The Creative Fire

A Dream of Eternity

I dreamed that a magician was playing with some red and green cubes, tossing them up into the air. Faster and faster he juggled with them, until all I could see were flashing colours.

'Why are they red and green?' I asked him.

'Red and green are the colours of eternity,' he answered.

The symbolism of red and green is alive and well in our own culture. At Christmas, we bring red and green berries and leaves into our homes, usually in the form of holly and ivy. They are a symbol of life springing up eternally, even in the dark depths of winter. The popular poinsettia plant also provides an elegant and more expensive version of this red and green contrast. In medieval poetry, holly and ivy were portrayed as opponents, as each struggled to gain mastery of the forest. And the Celtic story of Peredur in the Mabinogion describes a magical Tree of Life, one side perpetually on fire, and the other always green with fresh leaves. In alchemy too, we have the Green Lion and the Red Lion (also honoured in English pub names!), representing the vital forces of water and fire, the dual powers of nature and alchemy. They are twin poles, compatriots, but also combatants in the struggle.

Perhaps we would normally associate only fire with creativity, but in fact nothing can be created without using opposing forces. This means that within alchemy, creativity arises from the polarity of fire and water, springing out of their struggle and reconciling their contradictions. In all creativity there are usually two contradictory elements, and the creator tries to achieve something that is apparently impossible. For instance, you want to create something very light, but very strong. Most delicate or lightweight materials are also fragile, but you take on the challenge, and finally invent steel or nylon. You want to fly, but you must contend with the opposing natures of air and gravity; eventually, you succeed in creating the aeroplane which can overcome these limitations.

Creation is drama, and as my English teacher at school used to remind us: 'The essence of drama is conflict. But when you see a great tragic play at the theatre, you don't leave sad – you feel like dancing up the aisles at the end.' Great tragedy may harrow us, but the final resolution of its conflicts will uplift us. Although every creation involves a struggle, it need not necessarily drain your energy. You yourself are the third force in the battle, the one seeking resolution to the conflict of opposites, so you are not a combatant. I have already mentioned the three forces of alchemy, sometimes known as Salt, Sulphur and Mercury, or body, spirit and soul. We have been through the head-on battle in Chapter 4, but now the story takes a different turn. Because we have now reached the stage where we can go beyond our usual personal limitations, having experienced death and rebirth in alchemy, we are in a position to work *with* these opposing forces, rather than being in the thick of battle. The 'soul' force of Mercury unites the other two. The trickster nature of Mercury, alias Hermes, now comes into its own, as he has to find ingenious solutions and cheat the adversaries out of individual victory. As Hermes Trismegistus, he is often pictured as a wise old man, but he is also a mischievous spirit. He is quicksilver, speedy, elusive, humorous, and always ready to come up with the unexpected. Hermes, or Mercury, is often spoken of in paradoxes, and he himself contains the dualities that have been reconciled under his command.

My water and fire destroy and put together; from my body you may extract the green lion and the red... I bestow on you the powers of the male and the female, and also those of heaven and of earth... By the philosophers I am named

Mercurius... I am the highest and the lowest, the lightest and the heaviest... I contain the light of nature; I am dark and light; I come forth from heaven and earth; I am known and yet do not exist at all.

(From *Aurelia Occulta*, quoted by
C. G. Jung in *Theatrum Chemicum*)

So red and green capture the vibrant, shifting, spinning colours of creation, tossed in the air by the quicksilver magician. They are never at rest, just as the dance of creation and creativity never rests. The dream I quoted at the beginning of the chapter was a real one that I had many years ago, but I have never forgotten it, and have come to see that the strange message it carried has a lot of truth in it.

No one can tell you how to be creative; you can only learn how to go about the process.

Alchemist: Tell me, what am I to do with you? How am I to make you into the Philosopher's Stone?...
Mercury: Mr Philosopher, if you know, you can make it, and if you don't you can't. From me you cannot learn anything with which you have been unacquainted beforehand.

(From A *Dialogue between Mercury, the Alchemist,
and Nature*, Michael Sendivogius)

Alchemists did frequently drive themselves to the brink of madness and beyond in their lust to achieve the transmutation of gold. Chaucer wrote of smelly alchemists slinking through the streets in threadbare clothes, their eyes glazed from the obsessive search for the right materials to make their gold. One pair of alchemists used up 2000 eggs in a single, unsuccessful experiment, and struggled on for a further ten years without results.

In fact, when you are really working creatively, it is not a hard grinding struggle. You might struggle in the early stages, as when a poet or artist is still trying to find a subject. The worst part is when you cannot find any material to work on. Any writer will tell you about the horrors of 'writer's block'. There is the fear that a deadline will come and go without a single word being committed to the page. As far as an artist or writer knows, this painting or this book could be the last. There are never any guarantees of future inspiration. But once an idea is launched, it is thrilling work, even if it is difficult and demanding.

Everyone has the ability to be creative. There are many different ways to create, not only in the arts and crafts, but in problem-solving, business strategy, home decor, politics, teaching, and so on. To be creative means to come up with something new, but creativity should not be confused with originality. In the sense we often use the word, originality means being very individual, and different to everyone and everything else in every possible way. Creativity is the successful resolution of the disparate elements or opposing ideas in a form; it unites them, and reconciles their differences. But it may not be so readily attributed to its creator. For instance, you might admire a building without fully realising how the architect has brilliantly mastered the problem of achieving a sense of height and light in a confined space, using his resources and his problems creatively. An architect determined to be original, though, would have tried to make a really eye-catching effect that you could not ignore. And in the case of a really great creative achievement, it does not necessarily have the hallmark of the individual stamped all over it; it transcends the personality of its creator.

I sell Russian Lacquer Art, a very specialised art form, in which Russian artists paint fairy-tale scenes in miniature in glowing colours on a papier-mache base. This art has roots stretching back to Byzantine times and beyond, and its artists are highly-trained professionals. However, they do not strive to be 'original', and unless you know the art really well, you won't be able to pick out the work of individuals. Students train through studying the structure of composition, and through mastering its detail and ornament. Once the students have developed a solid technique, then they are encouraged to be creative and express their own style. But it is always controlled within the framework of the art, and thus strikes a wonderful balance between tradition and creativity.

This kind of creativity contributes to the collective wisdom of mankind. A willingness to transcend your own personal viewpoint is

needed if creativity is to flourish. The alchemists considered themselves to be privileged witnesses of the Creation of the Universe. They
saw the world come to birth in miniature in their vessels, and the
successive stages of creation unfolding in the colourful, dramatic
changes that followed during the alchemical process. In the end, pride
in one's own creations gives way to awe before the whole Creation,
forever changing, and forever being created anew.

Fire and Water

The fiery spark that sets the process of creation going is personified in
a number of mythological fiery creatures. The salamander living in the
flames in our emblem is one such. Many of them are birds, like the
well-known Phoenix, the bird of fire which arises from the ashes. There
is also the Simurgh, bird of Divine Light in Central Asian mythology,
and the Sun-bird of ancient Lycia, which takes souls and flies them up
to the sky after death. There is also the Russian Firebird:

> Suddenly, the whole orchard was ablaze with light, as if the sun
> had risen at midnight. It was the Firebird. The Firebird had
> come, with wings that shone like gold and eyes that gleamed
> like crystal. She perched in the tree, and began to pluck the
> apples with her beak of glowing amber. Prince Ivan tried to
> seize her. He moved as stealthily as he could, but the Firebird
> was quicker than him, and flew out of his grasp, leaving
> just one tail-feather behind in the prince's hand...The feather
> was so glorious that the king immediately forgot about his
> orchard. It was full of brilliance, like a thousand candles all alight
> at once.
>
> (From *Prince Ivan and the Firebird*, retold by Cherry Gilchrist)

The Firebird is the bird of inspiration. One feather from her tail is
enough to set you off on a quest. Prince Ivan is so inflamed by his
desire to find her that he sets off on a journey which leads to many
adventures. Fire can set us ablaze with enthusiasm. Sometimes it must
be seized with both hands, just as Ivan snatches a feather from the tail

of the Firebird. Sometimes the fire comes our way, if a feather of the Firebird flutters down before us. The craftworkers at Khokhloma, in Russia, who paint wooden dishes in red, black and gold, attribute their inspiration to a feather of the Firebird which floated down to earth there many years ago.

Once the fire is ignited, it demands energy, action and risk-taking. It can be easier to turn your back on the unknown, and stay in the cosy world of dreams and 'if only'. Fire demands decisive commitment. But it is not just for the chosen few – we all have the chance to find that spark and use it.

Fire is crucial to alchemy, because heat is a key agent of transformation. This is very easy to see in the context of everyday life, where heat is needed to bake bread, burn rubbish and dry the washing. Fire also effects colour changes, a critical part of the alchemical process. The artists of Khokhloma have their own special form of alchemy. They paint a background of silver aluminium powder on their wooden vases and cups, and when this is fired in a kiln, it turns golden.

Most of us have some significant early memories of fire. Children are fascinated by fire, and it must have been just as much of an anxiety to Stone Age parents as it is today to keep their children out of the fire. As a little girl, I was furious when my parents cut short my early alchemical project of building a kind of Aladdin's Cave in the embers of the sitting-room fire, which was designed to burn with different coloured flames ignited from varied bits of cellophane and paper. Curiously, although my parents were always nervous about fire, they were also fascinated by it. On at least two occasions as a child, I was woken up at night, and taken out to see buildings ablaze in the neighbourhood. The images of leaping flames in the darkness have stayed with me ever since.

Fire, as we all know, can quickly get out of control. Careful regulation of fire is crucial, both literally and in terms of our own enthusiasm. Regulating heat is certainly critical in alchemy, and alchemists have always been preoccupied with getting the temperature of the fire just right. They had no thermostats, and knew that too much heat could cause life-threatening explosions in their laboratories, as well as destroying the alchemical vessel and its precious contents.

So fire must be controlled; enthusiasm is a useful tool, but a terrible master, as it drives out discrimination. Other fiery dangers are haste, and the drive to push the work through to its end too quickly. In traditional mystical practices, fast results are usually frowned on. Any intensive and accelerated practices should only be undertaken by approved candidates under very strictly controlled conditions. Most teachers recommend slow and steady work, with an emphasis on the process rather than on the results.

It is easy to see that fire and water are natural enemies. Water can put out fire, and fire can dry up water. Fire usually works quickly, and water gently. In alchemy, both are important, and both must be carefully manipulated and controlled: fire can be brought back to a steady heat, whereas the pressure and force of water can be increased to wash through the material more vigorously, and circulate more actively. But the combining of fire and water is not exclusive to alchemy. Our own bodies are a miracle of fire and water combined. We are warm, watery beings. There are flows of blood, saliva and urine running through the various channels in our bodies, bodies which are in any case largely composed of water but heated by complex processes of energy conversion.

Chinese alchemy takes a mystical view of the workings of the body, and teaches that the alchemy within can produce the Elixir of Immortality, if we learn to develop mastery over the physical processes through special practices involving, for instance, breathing and sexual techniques. One tenth-century text gives a vivid, if obscure, picture of how fire and water are intertwined in the body, and suggests that it is through consciously combining the two elements that we can transform our inner state:

> *The lightning of true water boils and thunders in the realm of metal*
> *   and of water;*
> *True fire arises from Mount Kunlun – these are our yin and yang.*
> *The two restored and harmonized in proper ways*
> *Make the elixir grow naturally, pervade the body with its fragrance.*

The strong connection between fire and water is also found in the tale of *Prince Ivan and the Firebird*. The hero gets into all kinds of trouble, and is largely helped out of it by the Grey Wolf, who becomes his companion after first eating the prince's horse. Grey Wolf is a shape-changing figure, a trickster just like Hermes. Like the mercurial force in alchemy, he finds a way out of impossible situations. But when the prince is killed by his own jealous brothers, Grey Wolf can do nothing himself. Instead, he sends the ravens to fetch the Waters of Life and Death. These waters restore the prince, healing his dismembered body, so that he can finally ride back in triumph to the palace. There he claims his bride, who has been abducted by one of the wicked brothers, and is re-united with the Firebird, also stolen from him after he tracked her down. Fire initiates and inspires his quest, but when fire has finally burnt out, his life can be renewed by water.

Water brings healing, and its patient, gentle nature soothes away the scorching of fire. Water connects and lubricates. It smoothes away differences, just as a stream rounds a pebble, and it fills up empty spaces, finding its own level in all containers. Water is also a part of our psyche as well as our physical world: think how often we use 'watery' images in everyday speech, such as 'Relief flooded through me', 'It washed away my troubles', 'She dissolved into tears', and so on. One important characteristic of water is that it flows, and if we put this in psychological terms, this watery flow is akin to the current of our feelings and dreams. The source arises deep in the depths of the psyche; it is very difficult to make out where those feelings come from. But from the wonderful watery outpouring of dreams, fantasies and feelings, the creative mind can extract valuable material.

In the city of Bath where I live, the famous hot springs produce a flow of over a million litres of water a day. Those springs, laden with minerals, are responsible for the whole history of Bath, from its pre-historic origins as a sacred site to the grand Crescents and ballrooms built to accommodate eighteenth-century seekers after health and pleasure. But despite all scientific advances, no one yet knows exactly where the waters come from; the best answer is that the source probably lies deep in the rocks some 25 miles away from Bath. We can imagine the wonder of early man coming across this never-ceasing bubbling of hot, steamy water in the heart of a river valley. Here are water and fire combined as in alchemy, and this natural miracle ensured that the place became a centre of worship, sacred to ancient man long before the Romans arrived and built their temples and baths. In my garden, which has a view over the centre of Bath, flint tools from the Palaeolithic period have been found. I like to imagine the old hunter-gatherer tribes sitting on this hillside, gazing down towards the steamy marshes, which were even then pulsating with an inexhaustible supply of hot water.

Exercise 1: Following the Firebird

Picture the Firebird as vividly as you can. The Russian version has a long, pheasant-like tail, and brilliant, flame-coloured feathers that radiate light. However, you can create your own version of the Firebird. If possible, draw it, and give it fire colour with paints, pastels etc.

When you are familiar with the image, do a visualisation. Sit relaxed but upright, eyes lightly closed. Bring the Firebird to mind, and hold its image there for a couple of minutes. Now ask the Firebird to take you on a journey. What do you see? What places do you visit? Do you have any adventures on this journey? When you have gone far enough, or when your journey reaches a natural end, ask the Firebird to return you to the place that you started from.

What did you see and learn on your journey? Can you relate it to your quest?

Exercise 2: A Song for Water

Create a song for water. There are no excuses – everyone can sing or play a few notes. Prepare by spending some time with running water, which can be as romantic as sitting by a fast-flowing stream, or simply turning on the bath tap and paying it some attention. Listen to the noises of water, wherever you hear them, in the rain, the bathroom, the river and so on. Listen to some watery music if you like, such as Debussy's *La Mer* or Schubert's *Trout Quintet*, to get a feel of what such music can be. But don't feel that you have to produce something of similar quality!

Your own song can be as free or as structured as you like. It can have words, or not. It can be melodic or chanted, improvised or noted down. You can remember and record it for future use, or you can give it your all just this once. Whatever you choose, it is to be a celebration of water.

Uniting Fire and Water: the Key to Creativity

I knew a musician who suffered from extreme mood swings. He was an extremely talented pianist, but he could also be very difficult. One night I had a short, but revealing dream about him, which helped me to understand him better. In the dream, he was standing by a lake, watching a robot wrestling with a dragon in the water.

It seemed an odd image on the face of it, but after some reflection I realised that the dragon represented fire – his fiery passion to create – and the robot in the lake signified the mechanical, repetitive practice he had to go through. This battle is particularly relevant to musicians. Professional concert pianists have to practise for up to eight hours a day, working their fingers over and over again on the keyboard. The combination of robot and water was strange, but thinking of water mills, paddle steamers and engines driven by steam and water, it began to make more sense. They all harness water for repetitive action.

The tussle between creativity and practice can be harsh, and can produce emotional volatility in a sensitive person. Although piano-playing sounds effortless to the listener, this apparent ease is hard won by the player. The fire of enthusiasm and inspiration alone is not enough. Lengthy practice helps to turn the separate, almost mechanical notes, into a living stream of music. The arpeggios and scales that the pianist practises are composed of separate notes, but once mastered, they emerge as an unbroken ripple of notes. Repetition helps to generate a flow in other contexts too. Think of the way a child practises handwriting, at first very slowly and painstakingly, producing wobbly, distorted letters. Again and again she tries, until she develops a flow and can write words with ease. If you want to get in touch with this experience again, try learning a new alphabet such as Hebrew or Russian and practise writing out words in it.

Repeating also helps to purify, which is part of the alchemical process. My first meditation teacher used to set his class a puzzle. If you have a little puddle of dirty water, how do you get rid of it? By this puddle, he meant the natural condition of our minds, choked up with emotional debris. The answer was to add lots and lots of water. You wash that water through the mind every time you sit down to meditate, and ultimately, the impurities will be lost in the volume of clean, clear water and be practically untraceable. Homoeopathy works also with this principle of transformation through purification, by diluting and diluting the basic substance of the remedy until, by normal testing methods, no trace of it is left; in homoeopathic terms, what is left is a 'potentised remedy' which operates on a higher and subtler level. The gross level of matter has been removed, releasing its healing energies.

Alchemy teaches that miracles can be achieved by repetition. You must be prepared to wash your material a thousand times over if necessary. Patient, conscious repetition can lead to transformation in many areas of life. I have worked with the voice intensively at various times in my life, both teaching and performing as a singer. I learnt that certain exercises take a long time to get results. But when the results come, they may come suddenly and dramatically. A whole range of top notes open up – a new tone flows into the voice – power surges through a single held note. The singer may be astonished at the results. She may even be fearful, because the new voice seems to come from somebody different altogether.

There is no one certain recipe for creativity. But knowing the power of this duality of fire and water, passion and imagination, enthusiasm and patience, flame and flow, will certainly help you to open to your creative potential. A readiness to learn discipline and technique, dull though it is, will stand you in good stead for years. A willingness to repeat your attempts may bring about a complete creative transformation.

Exercise 3: Playing with Mermaids

This is rather like trying to find lightning underwater, as the Taoist manuscript described it. You are going to practise searching your dreams and daydreams for inspiration by way of a visualisation.

All the tempting ideas and notions that you come across, all the evocative feelings and nostalgic memories that arise are like mermaids or mermen swimming in the waters. They all want to seduce you and claim your attention. But you cannot follow them all, and most of them are insubstantial. They will melt away when you approach them.

Imagine yourself swimming underwater, surrounded by beautiful mermaids or handsome mermen, according to your choice (not necessarily a sexual choice, but see which ones you feel happiest encountering). You feel light and buoyant, and can easily turn in any direction. Your mermaids (or mermen) are doing their best to appeal to you, welcome you, claim you, but you are just going to look them all over in a leisurely way. Note any one mermaid that has more of a gleam to it. We are looking for a kind of underwater glow, like an eerie phosphorescent gleam, because this signifies that she partakes both of the world of water and of fire. When you find one who has this, approach her and lead her firmly by the hand up to the surface. Then ask her for her story, or to show you something special. When she has communicated something to you, release her back into the water. What are you left with? What can you do with this knowledge?

This is an exercise of fantasy, but it can help to train the process of sifting through the immeasurable number of drifting thoughts, feelings and images that we have, and being alert to one that might have some real creative potential.

Exercise 4: Working Creatively
Identify a small problem or situation that needs a practical but creative solution. Try to find opposing forces in it, which make it a challenge, and figure out creative ways of how they can be reconciled. For instance, you might have a room in your home that you would like to improve. What are the problems there, and how can you resolve them? Perhaps you want to make more space in a room, but you don't want to throw out your main pieces of furniture. Maybe you'd like to use light colours, but you want a warm effect. What can you do? Allow the creative process to play in your mind before you make a decision. If you get stuck, try changing your

approach. For instance, if you usually work through images, write it all down; or if you tend to mull things over alone, ask advice from your friends. If you can, put your solution into practice and enjoy the sense of achievement!

He who tries to enter the Philosophic Rose-garden without a key
is like a man wanting to walk without feet.

Chapter Eight

The Perfect Flower

I hope that you, the reader, are not quite as uncomfortable as the man in this picture, who has no feet. He is definitely an outsider, and can't get into the Philosophic Rose-garden unless he can unlock the door. You must understand this as a symbolic barring, and ignore the fact that he could probably hop over the wall, if he acquired some lower limbs.

> *The Garden of the Wise o'erflows with flowers,*
> *But ever is the gateway bolted shut:*
> *A thing despicable's the only key,*
> *Without which you will stumble, legless, on.*
> *You'll climb in vain Parnassus' heights, who now*
> *Can scarcely keep upright on even ground.*

So even chatting to the Gods and Muses, who are shown pleasantly whiling away the time on a little Mount Parnassus, will not enlighten our seeker. It's a pointed reminder that all the intellectual learning in the world won't help unless you can get to the heart of the teaching.

The alchemists really believed in the value of study, providing that it was approached in the right way. Study and inner development go hand in hand. Their traditional learning process consisted of three vital ingredients: contact with a living teacher, study of alchemical texts and, most important of all, alchemical experiments. Not everyone had easy access to the first two ingredients, but the third factor of personal work was crucial. Alchemists knew that you couldn't work entirely by the book – indeed most alchemical authors took pains to scramble their texts, littering them with allusions to great secrets that they could not reveal.

> Because this art was revealed by God… it is the duty of all Sages not to reveal it to any unworthy person… the Sages have expressed their knowledge in mysterious terms… The books of our Sages are only for the Sons of Knowledge.
>
> (*The New Pearl of Great Price*, Peter Bonus)

But whether you called yourself a son of knowledge or not, it was important at least to make the effort, scouring the texts for clues, and wrestling with their obscure utterances. To rub salt into the wound, these authors also told you that it was all quite easy really: 'Knowledge is one, as truth is one; and let me add that our knowledge and our truth are both very simple and straightforward' (*ibid*).

The aspiring alchemists certainly held the old masters in great reverence. This was not just for their legacy of treatises and illuminations, but also because through them one might tap into the living lineage of alchemy. The teaching was said to go back through the past masters of alchemy to Hermes Trismegistus himself, or even to Moses and Adam.

Entering the Rose-garden

The work outlined in this book is of a kind that you can initiate yourself, and apply in the context of modern life. To pursue this path, you need not be practising as a traditional alchemist. You may simply choose to add an alchemical strand to your other lines of work, rather than taking up alchemy as your main study. I prefer to call my own path a 'Hermetic' one rather than alchemical, because I work within the general field of alchemy and related traditions, such as Kabbalah and astrology. Alchemy is extremely adaptable. It has been re-invented many times already: the alchemy of Taoism is very different from that of the Ancient Greeks, and different again from the alchemy of Medieval Western Europe. Even the quest for gold itself is not central to all alchemical practices, since Taoist alchemists concentrated largely on the body, and the search for the Elixir of Life, and Christian mystics such as Jakob Boehme were concerned about attaining divine union, of which gold was only a symbol. There are healers, diviners, astrologers, ritual magicians, musicians, mathematicians and scientists among the panoply of alchemists, and all of them have approached alchemy from their own particular perspective, and used it in their own field. Isaac Newton, father of gravity theory, Claudio Monteverdi, eminent composer, and Paracelsus, founder of modern homoeopathy, are some of the alchemists whose intense and often solitary alchemical work directly fed their discoveries and creations in the outside world.

So you can follow alchemy as you will. But you will be able make better use of it if you understand some of the principles upon which it is founded. In my story, *The Quicksilver Way – An Alchemical Journey*, the seeker visits a large house where he finds two gardens: one is the place where he learns how to participate in the alchemical process, and the other where he understands the nature of the tradition.

Then my eye was caught by a trellised enclosure that seemed to be a small garden, judging by the leaves peeping over the top. I found the gate, but it was locked. How beautiful it looked inside! I could see clumps of purple wisteria in full bloom covering the trellis. I could smell fragrance on the air. I could hear rustling movements of birds, and a gentle running of water, as of a fountain... I shook at the fence like an angry child, and decided I would go in here, or nowhere. I sat down sulkily on the grass. I could wait.

There was a rustle in the grass, and I looked up to see a lady walking towards me in a long dress of light lemon yellow. Her brown hair was swept back over her shoulders, and she wore a band of pearls in her hair, with more pearls embroidered on her dress. She looked at me doubtfully.

'You come rudely, but you have a good heart,' she said to me at last. I felt that she had held up a mirror to my being, and that nothing was hidden from her. Her speech was rather old-fashioned, as though she had lived here alone for a long time, longer than one lifetime in fact.

'Enter if you please.' She took out a small silver key and fitted it into the lock. The double gates swung open to her touch. Inside was an exquisitely ordered little garden, with box hedges, flowers and taller bushes, all backed by the glorious vertical hanging garden of wisteria, whose fragrance permeated the whole enclosure. We had entered at one end of the longer side, and at the other, shorter end, stood a plain white stone basin. It was like a kind of font or very large chalice, opening out from an octagonal stone base and standing at about chest height.

(*The Quicksilver Way – An Alchemical Journey*,
Cherry Gilchrist, unpublished)

Alchemy has two guides: Hermes Trismegistus, and the Lady Alchymia. Whereas Hermes, as we have seen, is more active and mischievous, the Lady Alchymia is a gentle presence. She is not found so frequently in alchemical accounts, but she is related to Sophia, the spirit of wisdom. Sophia plays an active part in Gnostic creation stories, and is the personification of Wisdom as it occurs in the Bible. In this extract, the Lady Alchymia holds the key to the garden of alchemy, but she will only let the seeker in when she is convinced that there is truth in his heart.

This leads us to the nature of the key itself, mentioned in Maier's emblem 'a thing despicable'. Peter Bonus, having given us the frustrating news that alchemy is 'simple and straightforward', follows it with the advice: 'If you once depart from the unity and truth of Nature, you are involved in the bewildering mazes of confusion and error.'

We are told, then, that we need the truth of nature and also something that is overlooked and even held in contempt. Perhaps they are one and the same thing, and we already have the secret in our own beings. We can call it, very simply, awareness, and the truth of that awareness. This means giving attention to what we are doing, not functioning automatically. This was first explored in Chapter Two, but it is not just a technique that we practice at a particular stage and then forget about. We have to come back to it again and again. It means recording our impressions truthfully, not editing them. It also means keeping faith with our experiences, not denying or exaggerating them. It is a wonderful tool, which can transform what we do from dross to gold.

In terms of study, this means that stuffing one's head with facts and figures has little value. We've all met the know-all who can out-do you on your favourite subject, whether it's music, gardening, history or whatever. This person has read every book, knows every argument and makes your own heap of knowledge look pretty small. But something is missing – a real understanding of the subject. A person who loves their subject begins to embody it, so that their response is of the heart as well as the head. They can also use their understanding in daily life, and it may well spill over into other fields of application. The know-all is simply a type of human computer. And perhaps in a sophisticated world, the simple art of gazing, contemplating and responding truthfully is indeed despised. It doesn't make money or get things done in a hurry.

So approaching study with awareness means that you will respond to it with your whole being; it will feed you at different levels. It also means that you have a tool to discriminate between what contains truth, and what are just empty words. The truth of your own being is a touchstone which can sense the truth in whatever it encounters. Of course, this isn't always easy; sometimes we may have a subjective, emotional reaction to something that we read, or perhaps we are not yet ready to understand its meaning. But the practice of awareness, which includes observation and attention, builds up a way of getting beyond a personal response to the essence behind it. We are all composed of personality and essence: the personality is fickle, capricious and idiosyncratic, and often judges in terms of what will suit its own self-importance. The essence is the constant truth of our being, and although it is still individual, it links us through to the essence of humanity itself.

When I wrote my first book on alchemy, the publishers needed the manuscript very quickly. I thought I knew enough about alchemy to research and write its history without too much difficulty. I was wrong; as soon as I began to look into its enigmatic texts and labyrinthine history, I realised I was in deep trouble. I discovered that the only way

I could possibly meet my deadline was by ruthlessly discarding any material that was of dubious value. I had to find my own touchstone of truth, drawing also on my experience of other Western wisdom traditions. This helped me to dwell on the texts that had deep significance, and discard those which were little more than deluded recipe books. This taught me a very useful lesson, which was that I could and should use my own discrimination, not simply trot along at the heels of scholars who had gone before me.

Returning to the story of the alchemical garden, once inside the gate the seeker meets the greedy raven, and the beautiful but supercilious peacock, which are both emblems of alchemical change. But he himself gains nothing and sees no vital change until he becomes a participant in the process. The raven attacks him, pecking his hand savagely; his blood flows into the empty octagonal stone basin and there changes into a fountain of clear water. The basin itself turns first into a white, and then into a red rose. These are the alchemical symbols for silver and gold.

The seeker leaves the Rose-garden, but finds another garden nearby in the grounds of the great house he is visiting. This time, Quicksilver, alias Hermes, is his guide.

He took me towards a large walled garden. This had low gates which opened easily, and there were one or two people inside, pruning and tending the espaliered trees which grew around the walls. I could see at once that there were many varieties of fruit trees.

'These come from all over the world,' said Quicksilver, 'though most are saved from our own land. Here they keep the old fruiting lines alive, grafting onto them when they see fit.'

'For who?'

'For anyone that wants. Specialists. People whose trees have died and they need a replacement, but their soil won't take the old variety. Those who're interested in historic lines and want something from really far back that they can't find anywhere else. How many kinds of apple are there, for instance?'

I shrugged my shoulders. 'I don't know exactly – but probably forty or fifty.'

'Nonsense – hundreds and hundreds. And that's only apples. There are also pears, cherries, and plenty of other fruit.'

'But they can't all be grown here! There's only room for a hundred or so trees here.'

'And that's where the real discrimination comes in. You need not just specialists, people who can chart accurately, but people who understand the essence of species, who can pick out the vital strains from which all the others can be re-created if necessary, and from which even entirely new varieties can be created.'

I nodded, trying to take this all in, though I instinctively saw the sense of it.

It is not enough to have your own adventures, and your own experience of transformation. Or, perhaps that *is* enough for many people, but it is not the furthest that you can go. Alchemy takes you beyond the making of gold to the *essence* of gold, the Elixir which can be used to bring gold to life wherever it is found in latent form. For this, it is not enough just to subject yourself to the alchemical process; you have to understand it too.

One tree seemed to be very old indeed, and I spent some time admiring its twisted, deeply-scored branches which still put out a brave show of leaves and tender pale pink blossom.

'A direct descendant of the apple tree of Eden?' I asked half-mockingly, to disguise what was a serious question.

'Something like that. There's always one that's furthest back in the line. We have to reach back as far as we can, even beyond history into myth, and touch our deepest roots.'

As you look deep into history, you have a sense that there is one Tree of Knowledge, and from it grow different branches, different systems of teaching, with their own symbols and frameworks. All trees are part of one great tree; the fruit they bear is different, but they live and grow on the same principles.

There was a great range of variety in the shape and texture of the leaves, and the fruits, where they appeared, could be of drastically different colours, from solid custard yellow to brilliant red and green. Yet I saw that there was something in them all that was indisputably 'apple'.

(*The Quicksilver Way*)

The Tree of Knowledge

If we look at the underlying principles of a tradition such as alchemy, we begin to understand the pattern and the structure that it contains. A good book or teacher can help us to see this more easily. And then it is easier to understand other systems of knowledge, particularly ones from the same 'family'. Alchemy, for instance, is closely connected to Western traditions of astrology, Kabbalah, Hermetic writings, Gurdjieffian philosophy, and homoeopathy.

It is sometimes a wrench to turn away from imagery and personal experiences to a more objective approach, but it is certainly worth it. Studying geometry and number is one way in which you can get to the more abstract level of many disciplines. I am no mathematician, and struggled to pass my exams in maths at school. But when I started studying inner traditions, I found the interface between number, geometry and meaning fascinating. Sometimes I had to be dragged to it kicking and screaming, but once I was immersed, I felt that I had stepped into another world. It awakens the 'abstract' mind within us. This abstract mind is very lazy – or rather, we are lazy in contacting it – but once it is alert and operating, it brings incredible satisfaction. It is like taking a long drink of clear, cool water on a hot day.

We often think of 'abstract' as something divorced from reality, and devoid of emotion. But in fact it is the foundation of both emotion and logic. It is the root of meaning. Many spiritual traditions have a very clear numerical or geometric base, such as the Kabbalistic Tree of Life, which consists of ten circles connected by 22 double lines. This sounds very sparse, but in fact the visual symbol itself has great power. Each circle represents a sphere of particular Cosmic energy, and the lines that link them are pathways which can be explored through visualisation or ritual. The Tree itself is a map of all different levels of life; it can be seen as chakra centres of energy in the body, as well as a map of our inner psychology, and the primal manifestations of energy as spirit descends into matter. Many alchemists have been acquainted with Kabbalah over the centuries, and both traditions quote the maxim: 'As above, so below.' Everything we know in our normal world is a reflection of the principles that govern the entire universe, both in visible and in invisible ways.

The aim of this chapter is to give the reader some guidelines to work with, and also some material that may be useful in deciphering alchemy and traditions. The historical alchemist may have stayed locked in his laboratory, but you, the modern alchemist, are requested to keep your doorways open, to use your eyes and ears and find evidence of meaning in the world around you.

The Emerald Tablet of Hermes Trismegistus

The phrase 'As above, so below' is found in *The Emerald Tablet of Hermes Trismegistus,* a key text which we have already encountered in the Prelude. Alchemists believed that Hermes Trismegistus was a real historical figure, whose wisdom set the course of alchemy flowing. Although he was a god in the classical period, by the time his cult had evolved through the Graeco-Egyptian mystery schools of Alexandria, he was thought of as a kind of semi-legendary messenger and super-hero who had been sent to instruct human beings in the esoteric and alchemical arts. There is a whole body of 'Hermetic texts', known as the *Corpus Hermeticum,* which are mystical revelations of the nature of the universe, and many of these have only come to light in comparatively recent times. The Hermetic text which was known and venerated by all alchemists, however, was *The Emerald Tablet.* No one knows for sure who wrote it, or when; some scholars believe that it may be far more ancient than the earliest recorded versions of the ninth century AD, and that it might have found its way to the West from China or Central Asia more than 2000 years ago. It is a hard text to understand, but alchemists believed that it held the complete key to alchemical transformation.

The Emerald Tablet

True it is, without falsehood, certain and most true. That which is above is like to that which is below, and that which is below is like to that which is above, to accomplish the miracles of one thing.

And as all things were by the contemplation of one, so all things arose from this one thing by a single act of adaptation.

The Father thereof is the Sun, the mother is the Moon.

The Wind carried it in its womb, the Earth is the nurse thereof.

It is the father of all works of wonder throughout the whole world.

The power thereof is perfect.

If it be cast on to Earth, it will separate the element of Earth from that of Fire, the subtle from the gross.

With great sagacity it doth ascend gently from Earth to Heaven.

Again it doth descend to Earth, and uniteth in itself the force from things superior and things inferior.

Thus thou wilt possess the glory of the brightness of the whole world, and all obscurity will fly from thee.

This thing is the strong fortitude of all strength, for it over-cometh every subtle thing and doth penetrate every solid substance.

Thus was the world created.

Hence will there be marvellous adaptations achieved, of which the manner is this.

For this reason I am called Hermes Trismegistus, because I hold three parts of the wisdom of the whole world.

That which I had to say about the operation of Sol is completed.

(quoted in *The Elements of Alchemy*, Gilchrist 1991)

Exercise 1: The Emerald Tablet

Take this as your text for the next week or so. What meaning does it hold for you? You can try relating it to experience, to other sections of this book, and to the symbolism of alchemy in general. You will find it useful either to write the text out yourself by hand, paying it your full attention, or to learn it by heart.

This exercise is particularly good to work on in a group, where you can pool ideas.

Number and Shape

The symbolism of numbers is not arbitrary. The meanings given to numbers are based on their intrinsic nature, and how they work as dynamic structures. Of course, all this can be embellished, so there are variations in the listings of number symbolism. But by working our way back to principle, we can uncover real meaning.

Here is a listing of numbers, from one to 12. It is not comprehensive, and it is slanted towards the use of numbers in alchemy. You may notice too that there are 12 chapters in the book; often the alchemical process is described as 12 different stages. This list is given to help you approach the material in this book and any other alchemical texts that you read. You may also find it useful in other contexts.

One Oneness preserves the integrity of creation, and cannot be divided without losing its integrity. The alchemists talk about one truth, one matter, one process: 'One is the All, and by it the All, and in it the All, and if it does not contain the All it is nothing.' It is usually represented as a point or circle.

Two This represents two forces opposing one another. It often stands for male and female, positive and negative poles, light and dark, heaven and earth. In spiritual teaching, it can be used to represent the division between God and man, sometimes known as 'the Lover and the Beloved'. In alchemy, a separation from one into two is essential to release the vital energy that a polarity generates. Two may be represented by a line.

Three Practically every religious or wisdom tradition has a trinity at its core. The three ingredients of alchemy are known as Salt, Mercury and Sulphur, or body, soul and spirit. With the operation of three forces, we have a living and dynamic situation. There are possibilities for change and growth. Two opposing forces can be reconciled by the third in a new and creative solution. Three is commonly shown as a triangle.

Four stands for the four elements of earth, water, fire and air, the 'building blocks' of creation. Four signifies two sets of polarities, but although this creates tension, this tension can be used to build a house, for example, or to lay out an arena for action, such as a football pitch. It can also create an enclosed area such as our Philosophic Rose-garden. There are always battles where four is involved, but there is also the potential for constructive work. The usual representation of four is the cross or the square.

Five stands for dynamic focus, a combination of two and three. It can be sparkling, sexual or charismatic, or on the other hand, a decisive act of destruction. It can also represent the quintessential element which is a distillation of all four basic elements. A five-pointed star, the pentagram (five points joined by one line) or a pentagon (a five-sided figure) are its main representations.

Six is the principle of reconciliation. In alchemy, it represents the union of fire and water, brought into a harmonious relationship. Six is shown as a hexagon, or a six-pointed star made up of two interlaced triangles, which point above and below, uniting heaven and earth.

Seven signifies a full range of differences. It contains diversity within a recognisable order, like the spectrum of colours in the rainbow. The seven days of the week are an everyday version of this, each day with its own character. Something that has seven components in it has an identity of its own, over and above the individual ingredients. For this reason, a group is said to function only when it has seven members or above. The warring fours and harmonious threes find their first conjunction here, their sum equalling seven. Seven has no especially notable geometric forms.

Eight stands for the octave. It is also the number of architecture and structure, where two sets of four can be combined elegantly together. The steps of the octave, which we associate primarily with the notes in music, are said to represent a cosmic order, in which you find a similar note at the top to that at the bottom, but at a different pitch or level. The octave is generally seen as a 'vertical' structure. Eight is found as the octagon, and is the basis for much Islamic geometric art. It can also be seen as two interlaced squares, or an eight-fold star.

Nine equals three times three. In mythology we often find an original trio who have expanded to nine, such as the Greek Muses. Each point of the triangle can generate another triangle. Nine has an expansive, lively form of energy, that can include detail and diversity expanded from the basic three. Representations of nine usually combine the three triangles in some way.

Ten has great numerical significance as we go into double figures at this point. Although this may be in part due to our current system of counting (the Babylonians based their mathematics more on the number six, for example), it is still a natural ceiling for the first 'ladder' of numbers. It has stability. It is the number of the Kabbalistic Sephiroth, the ten principles of creation which manifest themselves in different forms of energy. Ten is not easily recognised when drawn as a ten-sided geometrical shape.

Eleven seems to give little scope for interpretation, although it holds a powerful intermediate position between the two 'completing' numbers of ten and twelve. Being ten plus one, it can occur as a group of ten with a leader or as a circle of ten around a central point.

Twelve rounds off all basic variations, combining them in one harmonious, comprehensive whole. It is the sum of three and four, and in astrology occurs as the 12 signs of the zodiac, which are the complete series of variations on the basic components of the horoscope (known as the quadruplicities and triplicities). Twelve is frequently found in myth and tradition, such as in the 12 Knights of the Round Table. Each represents a different viewpoint, contained in a 12-fold mandala. It's common to depict 12 as a circle – think of the clock face, for example, and the horoscope.

Exercise 2: Number Associations

You will be able to add many associations and links of your own to this listing of numbers and their meanings. You can follow the magpie approach – gleaning and storing up notes under each number heading. But it is also worth trying to understand how number operates in your own life.

● Whenever you find yourself in a group of people (12 or less), see what kind of dynamic operates. Does it fit in with the kind of dynamic I've suggested?

● Look at the structure of everyday items all around you, large and small. What numbers or geometric forms are they based on? Why?

Symbol and Colour

Many of the symbols we use arise from a number and its geometric form. The magician's wand represents a current of power, generated by the polarity of its two ends. The four-fold cross stands for suffering, spirit pinned down into the structure of matter, and the Round Table for inclusion of all representatives.

We can colour the basic form, which brings it closer to being an image, although colour itself is harder to give a fundamental meaning to. One society uses black to symbolise mourning, for instance, while another uses white. Sometimes colour symbolism comes from a natural source, but can still be interpreted in different ways. Red, for example, can stand for blood, but that itself can have different connotations – pain, boldness or energy, for example. Whatever colours you use, they should make some sense, at least in the framework that you are using.

Black, white and red are the fundamental colours of alchemy. Black is usually the Prime Material, and the 'death' of the matter in the vessel, whereas white represents the purification and rebirth of the matter. Red represents the perfection of gold, and the completion of the Great Work.

When we begin to put together numbers, symbols and colours, we get all kinds of interesting devices such as flags, badges, coats of arms, ritual symbols and so on. The alchemists were great symbol constructors, some of which were incredibly elaborate. But although people often imagine that symbols are confined to esoteric practices, in fact they are to be found all around us. One of the best descriptions of a newly-created symbol comes from an in-flight magazine that I picked up on an aeroplane, giving details of the new flag of Uzbekistan.

The flag consists of three horizontal stripes: blue, white and green. Along the edges of the white strip, the middle section of the flag, there are two red stripes. On the top, left-hand side of the blue section is a half-moon and twelve white five-pointed stars. The blue symbolises the endless sky and water as one of the main sources of life. The white in the flag represents peace, associated with both daylight and angels. Green means the renewal of nature. For many nations it symbolises youth, hope and vigour. The red lines symbolise the abundant force of life passing through the veins of the living body. The half moon is connected to Islam and can be considered as a symbol of Uzbekistan's newly found independence. The stars symbolise divinity, the twelve stars on the Uzbek flag represent the provinces of Uzbekistan.

Exercise 3: Looking for Symbols

Look out for symbols, crests, flags, and so on, in the world around you. What can you make of them? Can you see how their construction originates? If you find one that intrigues but baffles you, try to track down its source and find out how it was put together.

Exercise 4: Make Your Own Symbol

Design a flag or coat of arms of your own. Use the number symbolism given above as a guide. You will need to use your imagination and your sense of colour. When your design is complete, jot down some notes about its construction, similar to the example given above.

Lock the tree with the old man in a bedewed house,
and by eating of its fruit he will become young.

Chapter Nine

* * * * * * * * * * * * * * * * * *

Eating Apples

The belief that we can grow young again is found in many myths and tales. In certain stories apples, the sacred fruit of the Gods and of the Otherworld, are also the magical fruit of immortality.

> A certain king grew very old and lost his sight. One day he heard that far, far away, at the ends of the earth, was a garden with the apples of youth and a spring with the water of life. If an old man were to eat of the apples, he would grow young again, and if the water were rubbed on a blind man's eyes, he would regain his sight.
>
> (*The Apples of Youth and the Waters of Life*, Russian Fairy Tale)

As in most fairy tales, everything is possible, but nothing is that simple. The king does renew his youth, but only after his son has pursued an arduous and dangerous quest, falling into the hands of an evil sorceress, and battling with a many-headed dragon in the Underworld before he can find the apples. Youth, it seems, comes at a price.

Could alchemy ever really restore lost youth? Some alchemists faithfully believed that the Elixir of Life would be theirs, and that they could live forever. All they had to do was to find the right recipe, which was easier said than done. They were goaded on by stories of alchemists still wandering the earth several centuries after they should have died. But this certainly isn't everyone's goal. Prolonging one's natural life-span may be desirable, but who would want to live in this body forever? Still, as human beings we are fascinated with the idea of putting the clock back, or even stopping the march of time altogether.

But the question of life after death is another matter. It plays a central part in alchemy, in which gold is seen as the touchstone of eternity. Alchemy is not a religion, but like most religions, it is concerned with penetrating the mysteries of death, and opening the way to immortality. For the alchemist, transmuting base metal into gold is the same as the crystallisation of an unchanging body which is not destroyed at death. And as we've seen already, spiritual and physical work go hand in hand in alchemy.

As human beings, we are impelled to ask the big questions. Is there life after death? Can we achieve immortality? What is enlightenment? But we still have to work on the material that we have in the alchemical vessel right now, in other words our daily lives. This work requires patient dedication. It can also be very mundane. In the 1970s, I knew a woman who had been initiated into Tibetan Buddhist meditation. This was rather unusual at the time, but Tibetan teachings were beginning to attract interest, and they carried considerable mystique. She was the mother of several young children, and had a busy household to look after. Eager visitors often turned up on her doorstep, begging for crumbs of mystical knowledge. She would reply calmly: 'All in good time. First, let's practise sweeping-the-floor meditation.'

This was a wise answer, as well as a practical one. You could be told all the secrets of the Universe by a passing angel, and be no more enlightened than you were before. You might not believe them. Or they might cause you such dissatisfaction that you could not bear your present life any longer. More likely, you would simply forget them, strange though that sounds. The knowledge that we can consciously retain is directly related to our state of being, so when we are our everyday selves, we forget many of the deeper insights that came to us.

But the urge to seek out knowledge, rather than to submit passively to life, is very much in keeping with the alchemical tradition. In alchemy 'art takes over where nature leaves off,' as the tradition says. You can wait for fate to deal you its hand, but that is like waiting for lightning to kindle your bonfire rather than finding out how to light it yourself. Following the kind of work suggested here, or working within any good training tradition, will help to make real changes. As we change, we are able to receive more knowledge, and to channel it into our lives.

Some changes in our being certainly come about through life events, and you will meet people who are truly changed by critical happenings in their lives. But we can also choose to implement those changes more steadily, and more reliably. Through practices such as meditation, we can go deep into the psyche, and receive intimations of the realms beyond our normal human limitations, experiences which can then act as leaven in our lives.

So, yes, there is a way in which we can know eternity through alchemy, even if it won't turn white hair brown again. The work of alchemy can help to break down those barriers between our usual confined state of consciousness and a greater one, which transcends time and space. Those moments of 'knowing' will then inevitably have an effect upon our lives; this is a kind of Cosmic law. A person would have to make a huge effort to block out and deny the effects of such a contact. (There are those that do, some of them famous in their field, and they are often to be found on what might be called a negative path, pursuing endless research, writing book after book, all attempting to show that there is nothing beyond the scientifically provable world. If you hear their life story, you will usually find that they have had one highly significant spiritual or psychic experience, which they cannot accept on its own terms, and thus they struggle to reduce it into a manageable concept.)

In alchemical terms, this process of receiving sustenance from the higher world is called distillation. The vapours rise from the 'cooking' of the 'earthly' substance in the vessel; they ascend and then condense into purified drops, running down again to feed the matter that remains below.

> *In Wisdom's garden grows an apple tree*
> *With fruits of gold. Take it and our old man,*
> *Enclose them in a glass house, wet with dew,*
> *And let them stay there many days conjoin'd.*
> *When he has eat his fill of fruit, behold!*
> *The former old man is a youth again.*

This is the inscription accompanying the image, where it's easy to see how the 'glass house' corresponds to an alchemical glass vessel, heated over the fire. The tree described in this inscription may also have a special meaning in alchemy, and corresponds to certain chemical forms of metal which could appear in the vessel. Sir Isaac Newton, a closet alchemist as well as renowned scientist, wrote:

> I have in the fire manifold glasses with gold and this mercury. They grow in these glasses in the form of a tree, and by a continued circulation the trees are dissolved again with the work into a new mercury.

Exercise 1: Moments of 'Knowing'

Try to remember any moments you have had when you touched on another dimension of reality. What can you actually recall of the experience? Did it have any effect on your life afterwards? Was there something helpful that came from it that you can now renew, such as some insight or sense of direction? It might help to write it down in words, as the passing of time will often make it easier to express such an insight.

Contemplating Change

Here we have a somewhat bizarre image of an old man sitting in a glass house, eating apples in order to grow young again. Interpreting this in terms of everyday life, let's not think of it as a literal turning back of the clock, but instead as the renewal of optimism, hope and energy. We are at liberty with alchemy to wander between the worlds when we interpret its imagery, and to find a way of relating it to our own lives.

To take part in this process of renewal, one thing is essential, and that is the willingness to change. Sure, life is full of changes, and ageing brings change, but that's the kind of change that seems to advance without our consent! In fact, the more we age, the more we tend to resist changes, building up habits of comfort and thought and lifestyle. And this is not exclusive to the elderly; if you are over the age of 20 or so, you can be sure that those habits are already setting in. They just become more pronounced with the passing of the years.

When we give up accepting change, we give up on life. And maybe this is inevitable in our closing years. My mother, in her last years, wanted to slow the world down, and make it a place of as little change as possible. She kept more and more to her room, and lost interest in what was happening outside. But at the same time, something else was happening. Her memories began to play a very important part in her life. Ironically, as is often the case with old people, her sense of time began to fail, and her short-term memory was poor. But old memories that had meaning for her resurfaced vividly. Verses of poetry she had learnt as a child came floating into her mind again. She relived her courtship and marriage, and told me the story of her first love affair, which she had never revealed before.

It was soul-work. She was contemplating her life, ordering it, and distilling it. Even at that stage of her life, transformation was still in progress, and she ate of the apples in Wisdom's garden. For her this work lasted about 18 months, and when that was done, it really did seem as though there was nothing else that she had to do except cope with the increasingly difficult routine of simply staying alive, until the body itself gave out. On the last day of her life, I arrived too late to see her still alive. But instead of the gloom and despair I expected when I entered the house, I felt an overwhelming sense of joy and release. It was a beautiful spring day, with flowers bursting into bloom. In some curious way, I felt that she was at last free to be a part of that. The same day, I went to see the priest about the funeral service, and told him that I couldn't only feel grief, because there was such a powerful, joyful energy which accompanied her passing. We composed a service which included poems about nature, which she loved.

Alchemy draws its secrets from nature, and from our natural range of experience in life, it but works with them at a higher level. So the natural process which my mother went through is one that we can actively choose to use in our own lives now, without waiting for old age to bring it. The whole principle of taking a process that happens naturally, but using it in a distilled form, means that its potency will be greater, just as in homoeopathy the highest potency remedies are those with the least substance in them. (Incidentally, alchemy was responsible for perfecting the art of distillation and inventing brandy!)

We too can revisit the halls of memory, and become transformed by that. Through practising meditation, we can choose to go 'behind the scenes' of normal activity and contemplate the renewing, life-giving source there, deep in the darkness of the unknown. A poem I wrote in my twenties still expresses for me how this works – and it just happens to be very close to the image used in this chapter.

Now that the party is in full swing
Let us slip away,
Quietly away till neither an echo of laughter
nor a glimmer of light
Shall touch us.
And at the foot of the great tree
We will part, you and I.
Move away into the silent night
while I wait here,
marvelling at the dim-jewelled fruits of sleep
dropping from the branches,
till you return with news of gladness
in your face.

Dim-jewelled Fruits

We often have to go very close to the threshold of sleep to release our clutch on circling thoughts and internal chatter. Only then, when the quietness descends, can we penetrate a deeper layer of consciousness. Of course, it's quite possible to tip over the edge to sleep instead! Luckily, most recommended sitting positions for meditation require you to maintain your balance, so after a few seconds, the dozing meditator usually wakes up with a jump.

In the poem, I tried to capture the sense of being in two places at once – on the edge of sleep, and exploring the further reaches of the mind. Meditation is a kind of unravelling of the normal bond that ties together the different levels of being. Alchemy, along with shamanic traditions, says that we have all life forms within us. Our bodies correspond to the mineral and vegetable level of life, our personalities to the animal level, our conscience and love to the level of human essence; beyond that resides the level of the divine, which is within us although we cannot lay claim to it as 'ours' in the usual sense.

Alchemical transformation demands that we work on those different levels separately, before weaving the strands again into a new and harmonious whole. This makes great sense in the context of meditation. By meditation, I mean a practice which aims to go beyond words and images. A sound mantra or a visual image may be used as an aid to meditation, and so may breathing or even chanting, but these are used to absorb and neutralise the thoughts and emotions flying around inside us. They semi-hypnotise those levels of being, setting free the 'human' and 'divine' levels within us.

So the one who waits by the tree in terms of the poem is, more or less, the everyday person composed of mineral and animal levels. This 'person' is lulled into a state which often borders on sleep, allowing the 'higher self' the freedom to explore. Sometimes it is hard to get away from the normal circling of thoughts, but even then meditation still has an effect. We could say that our awareness is like a third ingredient here, which can move from one place to another. During some practices, that awareness is able to follow the 'explorer' on its journey, but at other times it seems bound to the commonplace workings of the 'personal mind'. Often, I can be caught up in my thoughts and fail to pass through them, yet those 30 minutes of meditation practice do not pass as a normal half hour would; there is still a sense of liberation afterwards, and I finish the practice refreshed, and in a different state of mind. The work of meditation continues as long as the meditator is sitting and following the basic practice.

Practising meditation is an act of faith, though, because it rarely brings instant or spectacular results. It is a slow drip process, the arising of misty vapour in the controlled, contained space of the glasshouse, which is then condensed into drops of pure water. These drops then trickle down again to nurture the matter that has been left below in the vessel. In other words, the process of meditation nourishes the normal, functioning self. All this is activated by the application of a gentle, steady heat that corresponds to the concentration of body and mind on the practice.

The glasshouse itself, the sealed vessel of alchemy, is very important in terms of meditation. When you meditate, you do so in a chosen and quiet place, where you deliberately exclude the normal distractions of everyday life. You switch the phone off, do your best to ignore the itch on your right knee, and gently put aside all the brilliant ideas you are bombarded with for the sake of going beyond them into the depths of consciousness. At least, that is the ideal.

Those apples that the old man devours as the dew condenses perhaps symbolise the process of 'devouring' your own experiences and emotions as they arise in meditation. In meditation, instead of dwelling on them, you consume those feelings and impressions, processing them immediately so that they are absorbed into the 'body' of the practice. The meditation technique helps you to do this; thoughts are subsumed in the rhythm of a sound mantra, emotions vaporised by the steady rise and fall of the breath. Holding on to an apple, polishing and admiring it, nibbling it and thinking about saving it for later – all this can obstruct your practice. Many is the time that I've had an absolutely brilliant idea during meditation, and have been tempted to follow it through in my mind. Not only does it really block the process of meditation, but it also tends to work itself up into a distorted form. Under the controlled glasshouse conditions of meditation, you cannot pursue thoughts or even emotions in the usual way. They can become over-heated and sometimes even do a fair amount of internal damage, if they are of the combustible type – self-pity and a sense of injustice are particularly explosive! But if you leave your good ideas and your highly-prized feelings alone during meditation, they will usually emerge later after the practice, and probably in a transformed state.

Meditation should always be taught by an experienced instructor, and even meditators of many years still have their teachers and checkers. You are dealing with some crucial functions, physical and mental, and it's important not to impair the way that they work in normal life. Careful supervision is needed, especially for a breathing meditation, since without guidance you can do yourself more harm than good. Meditation has a kind of objectivity about it, and it needs another person to help you establish that. It is always tempting to embellish the basic practice (after all, it's so dull at times!) and then you imperceptibly slide away from the main core of meditation into a creation of your own. So this book will not tell you how to meditate, but there are suggestions for taking a retreat which will also give you refreshment and a taste of what meditation is about, if you do not practise it already. There are also addresses at the end of the book for reliable organisations which offer meditation tuition.

The 'apples' of meditation are also real and tangible fruits; meditators are usually well-balanced, broad-minded people with an inner security which helps them to cope in difficult conditions. They still have their own individuality, whether that means they are fiery-tempered or placid, so meditation is not a form of brain-washing. Nor will it create perfect saints, washing away all defects of personality, though it may help to smooth over some of the rougher edges. If someone is practising meditation, it's usually possible to recognise the fact; one meditator often instinctively recognises another, even if they come from entirely different traditions.

Retreat into the Glasshouse

Although I have suggested that meditation should be taught live, not through a book, you can still find ways to take short retreats from the world which will have a similar effect. Here are a couple of suggestions for you to choose from.

Exercise 2: Regular Retreat

Set aside about 30 minutes every week, and if possible make it at the same time on the same day. Prepare a room to sit in by giving it a quick tidy, switching off the phone and turning off or taking out anything else that might disturb you. (Cats, for example, are especially attracted to meditation, and will probably wake from a deep sleep to jump on you if they are in the same room!)

Choose a comfortable sitting position, either on an upright chair or on the floor. You can support your lower back with a cushion, but leave the upper back free.

For the first ten minutes, just allow yourself to settle down. Relax, and let the breathing quieten. Check for tension in your body, and release it. Keep your eyes open but in a relaxed way. You can look around you if you like, but only very gently. Become aware of any sounds or sensations that come your way, but don't dwell on them. Let them flow through you. Be aware also of the space behind you.

For the next ten minutes, close your eyes. Keep to your sitting position, and keep any body movements absolutely minimal. Allow your mind to settle down even deeper. As you become aware of thoughts or feelings, let those flow on their way too. Try not to go with them, but on the other hand do not try to block their arising or their flow.

For the final ten minutes, try to include both inner and outer in your awareness. Open your eyes again. Let your gaze wander if you like, but without moving your head. Increase the sense of space around you where you are sitting. Recall the immense space within, and allow both to co-exist.

Finish by getting up, moving around, and then leaving the room to do something very ordinary if possible.

Note: the timings given here are only approximate. You can have a clock or watch if you like to check the different phases, and with experience you will find it quite easy to gauge how long you have been sitting for.

Exercise 3: Day Retreat

Plan a short retreat, preferably a whole day. You can do this at home, provided you can cut off your connection with the outside world for a day. Or you can go to a suitable centre, mountain hut, forest cabin or whatever, although the setting doesn't have to be romantic! It's more important that you shouldn't engage in phone calls, TV watching, computers or the usual type of reading. You could choose some source texts to read, either from alchemy or from another spiritual tradition. Plan out your day with times for eating, times for quiet reflection, for reading these texts, and so on. Plan meals which are either ready-prepared, or which can be got ready very easily. You could do some light tasks, but restrict this to one or two sessions, and don't use it as a way of catching up on all those jobs that have been piling up! You can have pen and paper to write down your thoughts if you like, or just to copy out some of your favourite passages from the texts you're reading.

Do everything with attention, but don't over-concentrate. If you want to go to sleep for a short while, or have a bath, that's fine. At the end of the day, write down your impressions of your retreat.

It's possible to do this as a group exercise, but this needs more careful planning and stronger discipline. For instance, you have to decide in advance whether talking will be allowed, and when, and if it should be restricted to essential communication.

Apples of Memory

In Chapter 2, I spoke of the need to re-process our memories. Earlier in this chapter as well, I mentioned the way that some of this work can be done in the last stage of life. Memory is a living thing, and essential to our being. Some brain specialists believe that memory holds our identity together. Even our cells 'remember' how to form a body. On the emotional level this is precious to us. A friend of mine was in a serious car accident and lost the use of his legs. For a week after the accident, he also lost his memory. Later, he said that although it was hard to live without walking, it would have been far harder to live without his memories.

Memory contains our personal treasure that we have heaped up from experience. However, we do tend to be highly selective about which memories we regard as treasure, and which we shove into the dusty recesses as worthless or unpleasant. Remember that alchemy is all about digging in dusty recesses to bring out all the dirty, rejected material, for therein lies our gold.

We also love to cut and polish our gems of memory, throwing away the chippings and presenting our beautifully faceted stones as the truth of our experience. Editing experience – we all do it – can be harmless enough. You want to recall an incident in an even more amusing way, so that it will entertain your friends. Or you craft your tale of woe so that justice is clearly on your side. The caught fish grows larger in the mind of the fisherman, the meeting with your lover more romantic in replay mode. But what if we cut out some really crucial information – maybe that car accident was partially your fault after all, but you deny this because you've suppressed the memory of looking at your passenger instead of at the road. For some people, the world is entirely shaped by their selective memory, and is divided into villains and victims, black and white, betrayal and loyalty. Any seriously disturbed patterns are the province of the psychotherapist, but most of us do have the ability to distort truth to a degree. This not only promotes a false picture of the world, but it can dam up our creativity. Such memories get fixed into a warped frame.

Maybe memory is always in a state of change; it is always being processed, like the old man devouring his apples. Memories are living cells in our psychological body, providing different sustenance and illumination at different times of our lives. It is only if we block them, by editing or suppressing, that they can't carry on doing their job. At one point in my life, I used to have a recurring dream about a heron. The dream would start off quite normally, and then the heron would appear as a silent, malevolent presence. I could not bear its cold inhuman gaze, which struck terror into my heart. In real life, I am very fond of birds, and I do like herons, even though they have a slightly sinister quality to them, like prehistoric flying reptiles with slow wing beats and trailing legs. But the more the dreams occurred, the less I began to like them in real life too.

I was practising dream work at the time, which made it easier to become 'conscious' in my dream and direct the outcome. One night, when the heron appeared, I decided to confront it. As I did so, it changed into the face of a boy who had bullied me when I was a little girl, and its gaze became the cold eyes that were calculating their next form of torture for me. I understood that the heron had always represented this boy in my dreams. By seeing him in the dream, I was able to acknowledge our bully and victim relationship in a living form, and from that moment I was free of it. The heron never returned again. Energy was released, fear was dissolved, and I am certain that unblocking that energy allowed me to use my vision and imagery more creatively from then on.

Exercise 4: Remembering Backwards (Part 2)

If you have not already started this exercise which was described in Chapter 2, now is the time to give it a go! If you have already been working on it, as you follow the train of memory backwards, be ready

to respond to any jumping-off points, and follow them back to wherever they lead you. For instance, if you are remembering putting on
your pyjamas, and suddenly this reminds you of doing the same thing
on a cold night when you were camping out, leap back to that memory.
Then try to follow that camping memory backwards in the same way,
until another springboard of memory appears.

In general, the further away in time the memory, the less detail you
will remember of the sequence, although certain images may be
imprinted with almost photographic clarity.

You may also sometimes decide to see how far back chronologi-
cally you can go. But this will only work if you follow the proper
method of working. For instance, if you deliberately jump back to one
of your well-remembered scenes of childhood, this won't take you
anywhere new. If you follow actual memory backwards in your mind
as accurately and as faithfully as you can, it will suggest its own leaps
further back into the past, which will be more interesting, and more
likely to reveal buried material.

As before, expect to fall asleep on the job! The work will continue
while you are asleep.

As coral grows under the water and hardens in the air, so does the stone.

Chapter Ten

* * * * * * * * * * * * * * * *

Fishing the Deep:
Visions from Another World

Imagine yourself sitting in an alchemical laboratory. It is dark, except for the glowing of the furnace and the pale phosphorescent bubbling in the alchemical retort. Your gaze is focused on the glass vessel; you have been there for many hours now, and for several days have hardly left your little laboratory. The outside world has almost ceased to exist for you, and you no longer notice if you are hungry or thirsty. Suddenly, your perceptions shift. The walls are no longer pressing in upon you, but have become insubstantial. They seem to be moving apart, so that the shape of the room is dissolving. There is a kind of dull roaring in your head, and your perceptions, that were previously so sharp and focused, are now swimming.

Although your gaze is rather blurred, you notice that the fire in the furnace blazes with a fiercer intensity. But the bubbling in the retort is slower, with huger bubbles forming a pale glutinous mass, exploding like bursts of lava on a volcano.

And now the laboratory seems to be full of shadowy presences, huge figures from another world. Curiously, you are not afraid. It is in some way quite natural. Then a figure emerges from the strange assembly of beings that have crowded into your alchemical chamber. You still cannot see him very clearly, but you know that he is tall and winged.

As you gaze at him, his presence draws you to him, and all that was still solid around you melts away. You and he are in a vast universe together.

'Come,' he says. 'I will show you the secrets of your dreams.'

You are flying together over a landscape covered with deposits of rich, earthy colours. Sometimes there is streak of deep ochre, or a swirl of dark green. Terracotta, burnt umber and gun-metal grey make up the pattern, with patches of midnight blue. It is a paint box made of the earth itself. There are no other signs of life there.

'This is the world of earth and minerals. You are composed of this world, and yet you scarcely know it. Your body is grounded in it. Many try to flee from it, but the alchemist follows the opposite direction from the crowd, entering the heart of the metallic secrets. He scoops up the coloured mud and dreams of how he can create anew from it. He watches patiently for the slow seepage of coloured soils, the gradually shifting patterns which bring change into his life. He listens until he hears the muffled beat of the earth's clock tapping out the centuries.

'Here in the coloured bands of earth lies the distillation of all your memories. For now, you hold them in your body, and later they will pass into the fabric of the universe itself. They are already distilled from a multitude of impressions, so that one taste, one pang of emotion, one scent holds the key to your experience of, let us say, a summer morning from your childhood long ago. The essence of that morning is already a part of your being.

'If you understand the work of the earth, you can use it in your own process of transformation. You mine for minerals within your own memory. You understand that all is change, forever in a process of change, however slowly it happens. You can accelerate that change some-times, lightening your burden, and liberating the distilled experience.'

And then the earthy landscape is no longer visible. Instead, you are flying over a blue and sparkling sea, where a light wind is stirring the water into small foam-crested waves. In the distance, you can see a palm-fringed shore, and all around you hear the cries of sea birds wheeling.

You fly down, down towards the waves, and without a word your guide plunges you below the surface. Surprisingly, you do not feel the water as wet, more as a light, viscous substance just a little denser than air. Below the water, the words of your guide float effortlessly.

'This is the water that does not wet the hands, the realm of coral-dreams and the dancing fishes of desire. Look around you, and enjoy.'

You see a school of little yellow and neon-blue fishes swimming past you. In the rocks lurks a bigger, silvery fish, and strange eel-like creatures undulate through the water, parting around you as they pass. Then you notice an array of exquisite coral, home to scores of tiny brightly-coloured fishes which dart in and out of its branches.

'These are your dreams, ever changing, keeping company with the fishes of your desires. Many are beautiful but have no meaning beyond their own appearance. They process the debris of your mind, and give form to your wishes.'

The large silvery fish has swum out in front of you. It gazes at you with blue eyes that seem curiously human.

'Some dreams come from the ocean beyond your own small sea, and they will tell you what you cannot know for yourself. You must pay attention to them, and give them respect. Then they will unlock secrets for you.'

You look again, and see spiny creatures, sea urchins perhaps, or nameless shellfish, and know that they are poisonous. You try to retreat as one vicious-looking specimen crawls up to you.

'Yes, there are unpleasant omens in dreams too. But always see these creatures in context. They keep the seabed clean, and devour weak, sick fish that are useless to you.

'Now choose some coral – take it away with you into the world of air and fire.'

You select a delicate branch of coral and swim up with it until you break the surface of the water with a gasp. The coral hardens in your hands as it meets the fresh air. But it perplexes you. What does it mean? Where did you find it? You have lost your sense of the underwater world, and although you stare at the coral and wonder at its beauty, you cannot recall how it looked as it flourished below the waves. A few images stay with you – a brilliantly coloured fish weaving in and out of tall seaweed; a transparent creature with a multitude of legs floating by. You will do your best to recall your dream through this.

You are far away from the lagoon now, and the world has gone dark around you. Fire flashes seemingly out of nowhere, and there is a smell of sulphur on the air. Thick, choking clouds loom up and surround you. Then you are through those, and looking down into a fiery volcanic crater. You have no sense of scale any more. Is it the largest volcano you could ever see, or are you looking once more into the fire of your furnace and the bubbling substance in the retort?

'Your visions of fire blaze and fade like comets in the sky. They are beacons on a hilltop, a fire in a forest clearing, a flaming torch leading you through the darkness. Can you ignite them? Do they come bidden, or unbidden? You will have to answer that question yourself, through your own experience. Fire can light up your life, but it can also destroy it. Look into the pit again.'

You see faces forming in the burning lava. They seem at first as if they are in torment – but aren't they now the faces of angels? One of these faces rises up towards you, floating on the flames, and its haunting beauty etches itself into your soul. It shines like molten gold. You are silent in wonder at this moment of perfection. And as it fades, you know that this vision will never let you rest; you will have to try to capture it in your work, so that the same gold shines out of your creation.

The flames quieten, and disappear with a low hiss. You are suspended in air. There is no way to tell what direction you are facing – up or down – or whether you are even moving at all. A dark wind blows past you, but you can't see or hear anything. Something, perhaps a feather, touches your face gently.

You wake with a start, as a voice intones softly: 'The spirit blows where it will. Remember its quiet voice, and listen to it when it speaks to you again, whenever that will be.'

The winged being has gone. You are back in your laboratory, rubbing your eyes. Everything has returned to its former stability, as it was before these strange events occurred. But, wait! – in the vessel the phosphorescent bubbling has given way to a steady radiance, glowing with a multitude of iridescent colours. Ah! This is the Peacock's Tail, the harbinger of hope, spreading out its glorious panoply of dreams.

Exercise 1: Visualisation
Take a quiet few minutes to follow this sequence again as a visualisation. Let the guide take you to these worlds of earth, water, fire and air in turn. Use the keys I have given you of 'painted' landscape, tropical sea, fiery

volcano and fields of space to help you explore, but allow your own impressions to arise there. Write down them down afterwards.

Who is your guide? Who led you through these worlds? Was it male or female, winged or human? If it was not clear during the visualisation, close your eyes and summon the guide who took you on your journey. Will he or she conduct you to the realms of knowledge again?

Visions and Dreams

Alchemy is a tradition of visions and dreams. Images can combine different levels of reality; we know from our own nightly dreams that they can blend events, emotions and thoughts and create from them a string of seamless images. Alchemists have long used images in their illustrations to express the enigma and mystery of their art, and to include all dimensions of our experience. As I showed in previous chapters, the traditional four worlds of earth, water, fire and air symbolise these dimensions very well. Broadly speaking, and in human terms, earth corresponds to the level of the body and the senses, water to the flow of thoughts and feelings, fire to inspiration and energy, and air to the world of higher mind. Each of these worlds has its own realm of imagery, dreams or visions. One warning: do not take any of my descriptions as complete; they are merely tags to help us sense the quality they embody.

Dreams from the Earth

You are rooted here, in this time and place. The world of earth speaks about this, through dreams and memories. Memories are compressed over the course of time until they are like a paste pounded from different spicy ingredients. Think how one little sensory trigger evokes a place that you visited, or an episode in your life. The smell of smoky bacon frying in the pan brings back for me an exciting night when I was a little girl, and we camped out on a farm where they cooked us a glorious breakfast in the morning and kept a policeman's helmet hanging in the hall to frighten away the burglars. Melon, on the other hand, takes me back to a very different sort of evening, when I was six years old and ate the fruit for the first time at a friend's house. I liked the melon, but I lay awake in fear afterwards because we'd seen a film about King Arthur that day with lots of blood and gore, and I was terrified that someone would attack me with a sword in the night. Even now sometimes, the smell of melon signals 'Danger!' to me.

I have always found this kind of memory evocation especially powerful. It shows us that experiences are not dead and gone, but continue to live within us. We have embodied them. We cannot step back into the past as it was, but we can connect to past experience through this living essence of memory. Some traditions talk about the 'long body', suggesting that we have a different type of body that persists through both time and space. It may even be possible to go back further than our own individual lifetime through this 'long body' and into the memories and experiences of those who have lived before us.

Some dreams also come from the 'earth' level in us. Through them, your body may speak of its needs or ailments. 'Earth' dreams are often rather slow and ponderous, and can be physically uncomfortable. If your body has to process too much food, for instance, this can be accompanied by lethargic, heavy dreams. I once had a tedious dream about sorting beans into different colours, which surely related to a rich dinner that my digestive system was dealing with methodically. Maybe your body dreams can also shed light on existing illnesses, or give an early warning about health problems that are already brewing.

Exercise 2: Awareness of the Season
When you next go outside, be aware of the season of the year. Draw in whatever impressions you can from the air, trees, light, and so on. Try to sense the essence of it. Keeping that essence in mind, try to connect through this moment to another similar day in the past. If it's a crisp autumn day, for example, let it transport you back to another autumn moment from the years gone by.

Try this exercise several times over a period of days, and see if you can 'travel' back even further through these sensory memories. Let them re-awaken past experience for you.

A Sea of Dreams

The world of water, the tropical sea you swam in earlier, produces a fantastic array of exotic dreams and imagery. But while many of these dreams are beautiful, they are also ephemeral. We have an incredibly powerful imagination which pours out shoals of iridescent images, not all of which need remembering or analysing. But it is certainly worth catching some of them. This is the realm in which most dreamwork is based. By training ourselves to remember dreams, we have a chance of becoming aware of some of their more significant imagery. This can shed light on our problems, or provide food for creativity. You can find out what transformation processes are going on in your mind, and through dreamwork you may be able to accelerate those processes, or liberate energy that has got locked in, as I described in the last chapter. There are many good manuals about working with dreams, and psychotherapy also uses various approaches to unlock the meaning of your dreams. It's impossible for this book to fully cover dreamwork, but I suggest that you begin to note down your dreams if you aren't already doing so.

Exercise 4: Dream Recording

Practise first of all remembering and recording as many dreams as you can. Recording with pen and paper isn't the only way – a dictaphone by the bed is also handy. As soon as you wake up, try to grasp the tail end of the dream that was in your mind. It can be a slippery fish to catch, but if you can grasp a little part of it, you may find that more of it comes to light. You will find that your recall of dreams almost certainly improves with practice. Sometimes you may also wake in the night and remember dreams. It's up to you whether you are willing to wake up enough to record them then! If you have trouble remembering any dreams at all, try using an alarm clock to wake you up in the mornings, or get someone to wake you.

When you have become proficient at this, it's time to stop recording all and everything that you remember from your dreams. Survey your dreams each morning, but only record any that seem unusual or especially interesting.

Remember: nothing that you dream need embarrass or shame you. Peculiar images are especially worth noting. Don't dismiss anything at the moment that you remember it. It may seem more significant later on.

Keep an eye out for any possible alchemical content in your dreams. You have embarked upon a process of transformation, and the imagery is likely to reflect this.

Exercise 5: Lucid Dreaming

Try to become conscious as you dream. This is called 'lucid dreaming'. Some people find it easier than others, but it is well worth trying. Set yourself a task: decide that if you see a door, you will go through it. Set yourself a prohibition: you will not get into a vehicle in your dream. Set yourself a quest: find a flower in your dream, and smell it. These are only suggestions, and it's better to take just one of these to start with. Remember it every night before you go to sleep. You may need to repeat this dream command for several weeks before you can follow it. When you have managed to do this a few times, drop the specific commands so that they don't cause any long-term disturbance in your dream patterns. Try in general to be 'awake' in dreams so that you can choose what to do – face the monster, follow the road, explore the house and so on. This way, you are likely to experience moments of transformation – energy can be unlocked, a world will unfold, or powerful emotions will be unleashed.

The ultimate aim is to increase your creative dreaming capacity. You are not aiming for total control, so regard this as a playful activity, and don't worry if you don't get consistent results. We all have different dream patterns, and some people have much easier access to the world of dreams than others.

A word of warning: there are times when you need your sleep more than you need dream recall. If you find yourself tired or stressed by your dreamwork, don't hesitate to switch off for a few weeks and leave your dreams alone. Also, you may find that as you start to pay attention to your dreams, they become more intense or eerie. This is normal as you become more aware of the shadowy country that you are entering.

Alchemy and Active Imagination

Imagery has always been very important in alchemy, and the alchemists deliberately stimulated visions to unlock the secrets of their art. They sought out their images in dreams, and on the borders between sleeping and waking. They probably used the glass vessel of alchemy rather a like a crystal ball, and perhaps the flames of the furnace to stimulate the imagination.

Structured visualisation, also known as active imagination, is an important way to bring forth images. These images may have a deep significance. Rather like alchemical symbols themselves, you cannot usually tie them down to one interpretation. They are poetic, they are resonant, and they may contain both past and future.

Sometimes you know immediately that an image is powerful, whereas at other times you have to wait and see whether it will turn out to be relevant or not. About 12 years ago, I saw a clear but puzzling image of myself wearing what I knew was 'a blue travelling cloak'. A couple of years later, there was a major shift in my life, and I began travelling abroad extensively both for business and pleasure so that travel became a core activity in my life. This new phase could well have been brewing, but if so, it was another example of how imagery can communicate what is going on in the depths, that we cannot normally access. Interestingly, I have since found that blue is a practical and universal colour to wear when travelling. Like shape-shifter Hermes, blue can help you to blend into any environment or culture that you find yourself in.

You can visualise alone, but group visualisation is the best way to tap this potential. Whereas dreams are usually personal, images from visualisation can often be significant for other people too, especially if they arise during a group visualisation exercise.

Visualisation was little known until the 1980s, when it suddenly became a regular part of group work, therapy, and even among the clergy, judging by a sermon I once heard a bishop give, in which he dreamily recounted his own visualisation experiences. Twenty years earlier, he might have got the church authorities seriously worried, but now this has become a common way to explore questions.

Exercise 6: Visualisation Sequence

You are going to do a series of 12 visualisations, using the 12 alchemical emblems illustrated in this book. It's best to do only one at a time, so that you could run the exercise over 12 days, or if you are working in a group, you could do this as part of a 12-week programme.

Follow the sequence in which they are given in this book. Begin by looking at the emblem for a few minutes until you can recreate it fairly accurately in your memory. Then close your eyes, while sitting upright but with the minimum of tension. Now bring the emblem to mind. Let it become a real scene in which you are present, with colour and substance. Let it develop and unfold as it will. If you lose touch with it completely, just re-set the original scene again.

If you are working alone, don't go on longer than about ten minutes, and it's fine to stop earlier if you get tired or the imagery runs out. In a group, it can be sustained for longer, especially if everyone is going to take a turn recounting what they see.

At the end, open your eyes, look around you, and return fully to this world. Then get up, move about, and maybe have something to eat or drink to ground you again. You can then make notes if you like, and think about what you saw and learnt.

Fiery Visions

Most of the imagery we see is generated by the world of water, but each elemental world has its own voice which can speak through images, dreams or symbols. Visions usually come from the world of fire. A vision is steadier and more purposeful than a dream or visualisation. It usually has a kind of unstoppable quality about it, and it can intrude into everyday life – you can be struck by a vision while doing the washing up or parking your car. It does not mean that you lose your sense of reality; a vision is more like an urgent phone call that you have to take. You give it your attention, even though you know you are still where you were a moment ago.

Some visions are vast in scale, and inspire generations of people, like the Revelations of St John in the Bible, while others can be a flash of little consequence to anyone apart from the individual. Visions may not be immediately comprehensible, but they are generally clear in content; their images do not shift or blur in the way that those in dreams and visualisations do. There is often the sense that they come from a source outside oneself, from beyond the personal imagination.

Sometimes a dream or a visualisation can turn into a vision. I was once working on a visualisation of a journey, when it suddenly took a different turn. The flow of images gave way to a vision of quite a different order. I saw a tall, shining being on a hilltop. Around him wheeled circles of tiny angels. His presence filled me with awe. Who was he? As I asked the question, I knew the answer: 'This is Michael.' Although I was still seeing with my mind's eye, I felt that I was truly in the presence of the Archangel Michael.

On another occasion, I was leading a group visualisation. One man was describing what he saw, when the energy suddenly heightened, and there was a great sense of presence and yet stillness. He told us that a huge golden Buddha figure had appeared before him on the road. We all sensed the wonder of what he was experiencing. Not very long afterwards, this young man died unexpectedly of a brain tumour. It is dangerous to draw conclusions from this, but I would certainly like to think that the peace he experienced in this vision heralded the way in which he passed through the gates of death.

Exercise 7: Contacting Images

Think back to any key images or visions that you may have had. How did they affect you? Did their meaning reveal itself at once, or only over the course of time? Did any of them change your life? Make contact with one of them now, and see if it is still alive for you. What can it tell you at this moment in time?

Lighter than Air

In the world of air, images practically disappear. Sometimes communication from this level comes through as a 'still small voice', which speaks unemotionally, but with impeccable accuracy. Many years ago, I was woken up in the middle of the night by something happening on the street outside. I looked out of the window, and saw two men rifling through our car. 'They're looking for something to break into next door with,' were the quiet, colourless words that echoed in my mind. I knew there was nothing valuable in the car, and I'm afraid I did nothing. Next day, we discovered that these men had indeed forced an entry next door, and were subsequently chased off down the street by the irate owner – a sequel which, I'm ashamed to say, I slept through completely! This shows in a rather negative way that we are not forced to listen to this voice, or act on it. It can be hard to recognise it when it speaks, because thoughts pass through our mind all the time, and how can you tell one internal voice from another? Curiously, it's always afterwards that I am sure about the quality of this particular 'voice', and I have sometimes ignored it to my cost. 'Tell him now, and everything will be all right,' I heard this voice say also at a later date. I didn't, and it wasn't.

This brings us to an interesting point, however. These worlds of dreams, visions and insights are worlds of information. They are not commands, and we have the choice to follow their indications or not. We may even go against apparent 'advice' from these images and dreams, because they can only inform us relative to the present context. Humans are creators; we can break an existing mould and create a new one. Breaking the mould can be painful, but it is sometimes what we have to do.

Sometimes the quiet voice can bring comfort and reassurance when it is most needed. A young woman had just been diagnosed with cancer. She went out for a walk on the hills, to be in touch with the wind and moorland that she loved. She walked until she was exhausted, then sat down to rest against one of the old standing stones that been erected there thousands of years ago. As she sat there, weeping, alone and afraid, she heard the words, 'Don't worry – everything's going to be all right.' And it was.

Images of air are often scarcely perceptible. Sometimes they take the form of a presence with no visual image attached. This is not the same as 'ghosts', which can be described as the residue of a person's psyche, somehow trapped in our world. These 'air' presences are an experience of a world of beings and of consciousness beyond our normal perceptions, but sometimes accessible to us. Are these experiences of angels, or the illuminated minds of those who have lived before us? Are they beings living now, with whom we can communicate at the non-physical level? I leave the question open for you to explore. Just remember that all imagery is clothing. Our perceptions of reality are always an interpretation.

Exercise 8: The Back of Your Head

This takes only a few minutes, and can be done at any quiet moment. Become aware of the back of your head. Allow your attention to move from the front of your head and brain into the back. Sense that the back of your brain has its own rhythms, and its own type of consciousness. There is unlikely to be any immediate imagery or results. Learning to activate your attention there will have its own effects, and may open a doorway to a bigger world.

The Sun and its shadow complete the work.

Chapter Eleven

. . . .

Binding Light and Dark

The Sun, the pole's bright torch, can't penetrate
Dense bodies, so half earth remains in shade.
The shadow, though it seem a thing despised,
Gives much of use to the Astronomers.
To the Wise, the Sun and shadow give much more,
For they complete the art of making gold.

Now alchemy takes on a Cosmic perspective. We move from the
intensity of inner worlds out into the vastness of space, to contemplate the alchemy of our solar system and beyond. But does this
illustration only refer to this grand external scale? By now, we
should be rather more wary of attributing only one context to an
alchemical image, since in alchemy inner and outer worlds are
always interrelated. Maier's emblem at first seems to be about the
physical sun and its shadow, but from what we know already, we
can easily guess that these signify the light and dark forces of
alchemy: the dark slumbering mass of the primal material, and the
brilliant and enlightened alchemical gold into which it can transform. But this is not all; the emblem and its accompanying poem go
further, showing how sun and shadow also relate to the moon and
the earth, and how all are contained in a unifying starry circle. This
too is not simply to be read on the physical level. Sun and shadow,
the fundamental duality, interweave subtly with the trio of sun,
moon and earth, which we can recognise as the three types of
indwelling energy, known in alchemy as salt, mercury and sulphur.

All are contained within the circle of stars, which represents the completion of the alchemical work of transformation.

To begin with, let's explore further the connection between cosmology and consciousness, the relationship between the mind of man and the world outside. Then we'll move on to looking at the significance of sun and shadow, and in more depth as to how the three fundamental energies relate to human destiny and will. This helps to show how inner and outer are connected, which in turn increases our own flexibility to move freely between these worlds.

Imagine yourself back in the early days, when people did not yet understand the cycles of the sun and the moon. You would notice regular changes in the night sky, and in the pattern of sunrise and sunset, and you would certainly be familiar with the waxing and waning of the moon. But how it all fitted together was still a mystery. You and your fellow human beings yearned to acquire this knowledge. To understand the changing patterns in the sky meant that you could gain mastery over the unfolding patterns of life. It was the way to build a framework that would help you to count time, and to create calendars which could help you to predict the changes of the seasons. And so many thousands of years ago, prehistoric people began to construct moon calendars. Then, as their understanding developed, they built stone circles and megaliths whose alignments accurately corresponded with the solar year, and sometimes with the position of the stars. Whatever other function these monuments had in their society, it's clear that the people of the day wanted to relate their own lives to the cycles of the heavens. In the unceasing, shining dance of the skies they found a sharp contrast with their own mortality. But this contrast acted as a stimulus to develop religious belief. We know from early mythologies, those of Egypt and Greece for instance, that the daily 'death and rebirth' of the sun became a focus for beliefs about resurrection and reincarnation, which in turn gave people hope that they too could bridge the abyss between mortality and immortality.

By this time, even eclipses, those terrifying, sudden 'deaths' of the sun or moon, could be predicted. The cycle of sun and moon eclipses, which stretches over about 18 years, was finally discovered by Babylonian astronomers, and named by them as the 'Saros' cycle.

You may see in all this the polarity of sun and shadow at work, not only in the literal interplay of light and dark, but also in the way that it posed fundamental questions which encouraged people to explore the nature of life and death. Where contradiction and duality exists, we strive to find reconciliation, and in so doing we open the way to developing human potential. This is the way of alchemy as much as it was the earliest way of exploring cosmology.

Exploration of the universe went on. Although Copernicus proposed in 1543 that the earth went around the sun, and not vice versa, most people were still unconvinced at the time Michael Maier published his *Emblems, Fugues and Epigrams* in 1617. Look how prominently he has placed the earth in the centre of the emblem, and how large it is in relation to the sun. He has called the sun a 'pole' too, which suggests he saw it as a satellite of the earth. Or perhaps he was hedging his bets in the face of such fierce opposition, at a time when such radical new ideas could be considered as dangerous heresy.

But for our purposes, it doesn't matter if Maier's knowledge of the universe was limited. So is ours. Who knows what discoveries will be made over the next few hundred years? Our viewpoint will always be relative, never full and objective. Don't we still experience the earth as static and central in the universe, even though intellectually we know that we are hurtling through space? Perhaps we still have some catching up to do with Copernican cosmology. Even though it may take a long time to assimilate every discovery, the point is that each new picture of the world does offer us the chance to extend our consciousness. In the case of the solar system, we have the chance to move from a self-centred, 'earth-based' world to a 'sun-based' universe, rather similar to the way that a young child learns to recognise the independent existence of other people, and through that gains more interaction with them.

Discoveries about the universe outside us do help to develop innate human potential. They also bring further questions and doubts, which in turn spur us on to seek new knowledge. Surely Einstein's discovery of the principle of relativity has affected us profoundly. It has taught us to begin, at least, to acknowledge the value of other cultures and religions. In the light of his work, it is hard to believe any longer in one absolute standpoint. Even the current fundamentalist movements are in one sense a desperate and sometimes violent attempt to cling on to such convictions of unquestionable supremacy. A new perspective can be painful, and Einstein's revelations may have contributed to the current crisis of values, in which the old moral certainties have been undermined. At the same time, his discoveries and those of quantum physics have helped to create a ferment of creative speculation, for instance about the possibilities of time travel, of life on other planets, and of parallel universes. Science fiction, fantasy and fact are all mingling together in an exciting melting pot of ideas. This cauldron may also be the birthplace of a new spiritual understanding.

Alchemy has never had any trouble in relating spiritual and physical knowledge. As Maier's epigram says, the alchemist goes beyond the work of the astronomer. He or she learns how to use the inner sun, moon and earth in the art of transformation. As one fourteenth-century alchemist put it: '[Alchemy is] the secret of the mastery of fixing the sun in our own sky, so that it shines therein and sheds light and the principle of light upon our bodies.'

The sun and the shadow are the starting point. They represent the pure gold and the despised black primal material, the glorious end arising from a humble beginning. But in fact, these begin from the same place, as seen in the image of the tail-eating serpent Ouroboros. The alchemist is not content with the unawakened world of Ouroboros, however, but wants to transform its potential gold into bright, shining spirit. We are given the will to be creators, and we can sometimes, at least, take our destiny into our own hands. So first of all we must break down that apparent unity, represented by Ouroboros, to find the first substance, the primal material within. Find the shadow, and you will find the sun. Work with the despised, rejected and overlooked elements, and you will unlock the whole chain of the transformation process. Once the sun and the shadow are separated, a space is created between them in which the trinity of sun, moon and earth can be recognised, and the interaction of their three energies used in the alchemical process. And so finally, the slumbering serpent is transformed into a shining, starry circle. The serpent held the elements in heavy lethargy. Now they are released, transmuted and creative. They take their place within the Cosmic dance of the universe.

Exercise 1: Sun and Shadow

Look back over the exercises you have done so far. Can you identify the sun and the shadow at work there? What has created a blaze of enthusiasm for you (the sun), and what have you experienced great resistance to (the shadow)? Maybe they were two sides of the same coin; was there a relationship between your positive energy and your reluctance? Did you manage to get past their conflicting demands? If so, did you discover a unifying 'starry circle' which helped to make sense of the work as a whole? You can allow the poetry of these images to speak to you, rather than being too analytical.

Three by Three

Let's now move on to looking at the role of the three Cosmic energies in more depth. To begin with, I want to suggest how these relate to our deepest drives, which can be called 'the three motivations'. Then we'll take another way of looking at three basic modes of being, which are known as 'head, heart and guts'. Together these two sets of three form a nine-fold grid, which we can use as a basis for profiling the individual, and also as a kind of magical talisman for focusing our will.

These three 'motivations' underpin our lives, and underlie all our actions. But it is said that each of us has one primary motivation that helps to determine our approach to life, and defines some of our deepest drives. The motivations are in one sense impersonal, as though each person is created from an impulse of divine will, and around this 'motivation' his or her individual character is constellated. They are very powerful, and recognising the part they play in our lives is the first step towards working constructively with them.

In alchemy, we can call these motivations Seraphim, Cherubim and Malachim. These three types of Angels represent some of the highest Cosmic impulses, and although we shouldn't take these correspondences too literally, they do give us a strong sense of the type of energy that they embody, and of how this originates beyond our personal world.

Although what follows is a very generalised and brief description, it should be helpful in understanding the three different types of human being as they are governed by one of these 'angelic' motivations.

Seraphim

This is the 'active' force, symbolised by light and by fiery serpents. People motivated by the Seraphim are expansive, creative and extravagant. They believe that it's more important to create something than to worry about waste. This can also apply where love and money are concerned! They trust in the generosity of the universe, and are always ready to start again. They sense that the spirit is all around us, and everything in the world reflects the glory of that spirit. Seraphim can be artists, entrepreneurs, travellers or preachers.

Cherubim

This motivation is also known as the receptive or denying force. Its symbol is the dark vortex. It contains and controls whatever comes its way, so that 'Cherubim' people work through enclosing and shaping their experience. They can seem inattentive, and even detached from normal human concerns, but they are always working away on the inside. They seek out mystery, and try to find its hidden meaning. They discard external forms, seeing them only as shells. To find the heart of things, they say, you must get beyond appearances. Cherubim can be healers, mystics, researchers and spies.

Malachim

Malachim people love to communicate, and are go-betweens. As Angels, they are the heavenly messengers. They try to strike a balance, and bring reconciliation, not necessarily in the form of peace but by making a place where different types of experience and different viewpoints can co-exist. This applies to their own lives as well. They are fascinated by transformation and the world for them is a magical place. They are at home in both the external and internal worlds, and love the interplay between them. Malachim make good actors, magicians, writers and teachers.

These are only guidelines; we are all, to some extent, a mixture of all three motivations, so it's a question of trying to work out which one predominates. It's this one motivation that helps to give us our sense of meaning in life. It may also define the way we approach religion, and explain some of the clashes that spring up between people: an extrovert, evangelical Seraphim person for example would be anathema to the mystical and monastic Cherubim type.

Exercise 2: Finding Your Motivation

Which motivation you are most governed by? This is not something you can easily change. A person's prime motivation may possibly change during the course of a lifetime, but in general, it's outside our conscious control. Knowing it, however, means you can live with it more easily, and respect people of other motivations, whose approach may be very different from yours.

Questions you can ask to get into this puzzle are:

- What kind of work are you doing, and why?
- If you take part in rituals, what kind of role are you usually given?
- How do other people see you (even if you think they might be wrong)?
- What is your main drive in a relationship? Is it a blaze of passion and energy (Seraphim), transformation through union (Malachim), or achieving intense intimacy with the other person (Cherubim)?

If you are working in a group, you can think up some other questions to ask, based on these definitions. You might also like to find out more about these three orders of Angels and their traditional roles.

Head, Heart and Guts

The set of three we've just looked at represents an equal trio of energies, standing side by side, as it were. But we can also see the three fundamental forces as a ladder with three vertical steps, just as the alchemical trio of salt, mercury and sulphur moves from a denser material form to a more spiritual one. In reference to everyday life we can call these 'head, heart and guts', moving from top to bottom. These too can apply to individuals, so that one person is a 'head' type, and another is a 'guts' type, for instance.

Starting at the bottom, the physical 'guts' type, ruled by the body, is obvious – or is it? At this level lies a very particular type of knowledge that can be very hard to access. Here are the interwoven layers of the genetic code, of instinct, of the metabolism and its subtle, changing balance of hormones. The 'gut-centre' type of person is more in contact with this level of being than the other two types, more likely to act from instinct and to pay attention to sensory impressions. Although this lies at the bottom of the ladder, this does not suggest any inferiority. The knowledge of this level is just as valuable. The person who understands how to survive in the mountains, who has a rapport with nature, or who is a herbalist and healer, is no lower on the scale than the one who works with abstract mathematics.

The 'heart' level, on the middle rung, is where feelings and intuition reside. But note that love is present in all these levels; no one type has a monopoly on love. Love is a kind of universal energy in its own right, not to be confused with the normal gamut of emotions. At the heart level, we can receive direct 'information' about the feelings of others; we sense their pain, joy or sorrow. Someone who is centred at this level will be more swayed by moods, but will be much more sensitive to the state of other people. They show a readiness to respond to need.

The 'head' type is governed by the world of reason, ideas and thought. Analysis is the way forward for this kind of person, who can usually hold a multitude of facts and figures in mind. For them, words have power, and music too has a special place at this level. The level of 'head' also points the way to real abstract thought, when the mind understands shapes, numbers, and spatial dimensions with a kind of inborn comprehension. The 'head' person can usually step back from his or her emotions and give a clear, cool appraisal of a situation

We are all a mixture of these three levels, even though one tends to predominate. It is also possible to work on our less developed levels. The course of work in this book should help to unlock the potential of the 'sleepier' ones. When one of the other centres wakes up, the effects can be powerful. Remember that your sensations, feelings and insights are all very valuable information, but you do not always need to identify with that information.

Exercise 3: Finding Your Type

Which type might you be – head, heart or guts? Here are some lines of enquiry which may give you clues.

Check yourself first thing in the morning: whichever centre wakes up first is likely to be your type. If you are a 'guts' type, you wake up ready for action, whether it's to go to the gym, make love or just jump out of bed. As a heart type, you may immediately be caught up in a tide of emotion, reviewing your internal state and recalling the experience of yesterday. A head type is ready to discuss the secrets of the universe, check new email and read a paper. You may even do all this while still in bed.

How do other people see you? Ask, if you don't know. The framework of 'head, heart and guts' types is very easy for anyone to relate to.

Have you ever been swept off your feet by physical sensations or experiences, by emotions, or by powerful ideas? If so, then you are probably *not* of that particular type. You will tend to have more control over, and more familiarity with, your own favourite mode of action.

Exercise 4: Working on the Balance

Choose one of your less-developed centres and devise an activity for it. It can be something simple from everyday life. Don't look for some worthy project; treat it simply as exercise for some of your under-exercised faculties. Here are some suggestions to get you going.

- Guts – try out a new kind of sporting activity. Do some physical work around the home. Walk instead of driving or taking transport. Go camping.
- Heart – visit an art gallery and let the paintings speak to you. When you meet people, try to feel in your heart area what kind of impressions they make on you.
- Head – Watch a favourite film and try to get behind your normal response to it. Work out what's going on, and why you like it.

Try some puzzles (crossword, jigsaw, etc) or learn a complicated card game.

Exercise 5: Making a Talisman

This is a section of practical work. Follow the instructions step by step. Interpretations are given at the end of the chapter, so leave them till last!

Part 1

Make a grid of nine squares, three by three, on a sheet of paper. This is based on the idea of three vertical modes of being, which I've labelled as head, heart and guts, and the three horizontal modes, the motivations known as Seraphim, Malachim and Cherubim, going from right to left respectively. This gives us a kind of grid of co-ordinates, so that the square on the bottom left, for example, is Cherubim at the physical level of the guts.

You are going to make a talisman using this grid. You will be using your first grid experimentally, so don't worry too much about appearances. Once you have created this first one, you can repeat the same format, but with more care and in materials of your choice.

Take three colours, black, red and gold, which you will use to fill the nine empty squares on your grid, one colour for each square. You can use coloured paper, sticky stars or dots, paints or coloured pens. Or you can simply write B, R and G in the squares, but the talisman does need to be made in colour later if it's to be effective. The basic meanings for these three colours as used here are:

- Black: compassion, sorrow, suffering, the past
- Red: energy, present life, joy, laughter, beauty
- Gold: transformation, eternity, illumination, the future

Each colour can only be used three times, and each vertical and horizontal row must contain only one of each colour. Try to do this intuitively, without analysing your selection too much. There is no right or wrong, only your individual pattern on the grid. When you finish your lay-out, you should have a diagonal line of three squares composed in

B	R	G
G	B	R
R	G	B

G	R	B
R	B	G
B	G	R

R	G	B
B	R	G
G	B	R

B	G	R
G	R	B
R	B	G

G	R	B
B	G	R
R	B	G

B	R	G
R	G	B
G	B	R

B	G	R
R	B	G
G	R	B

R	G	B
G	B	R
B	R	G

R	B	G
G	R	B
B	G	R

G	B	R
B	R	G
R	G	B

G	B	R
R	G	B
B	R	G

R	B	G
B	G	R
G	R	B

Twelve Variations on the Grid of Nine

one colour only (i.e., three reds, three golds or three blacks making a diagonal). For interpretation of these diagonals, and what it suggests about your inner nature, turn to page 155.

There are six possible coloured diagonals, because each can slope in two directions. When you look more closely, you may notice that there are 12 possible types of grid, depending on how the other colours are arranged around that diagonal. So from a basic three colours, we've arrived at 12 different talismans, each of which may signify a different type of person. Although we won't interpret these 12 now, it is a potential profiling system, which you may wish to explore further. Most divination systems are built up in this way, developing basic sets of principles like this. The 12 signs of the zodiac, for instance, are created from a three-by-four plan, using the 12 possible combinations of 'cardinal, fixed and mutable' with the four elements. Aries, for instance, is 'cardinal fire', whereas Leo is 'fixed fire' and Sagittarius 'mutable fire'. Each of these combinations suggests a different kind of energy and drive.

Part 2

If you wish, you can now make this grid again, using your original design, but this time with the intention of fixing this pattern for future use. Make it with care and attention; you might want to use different materials, for instance, to give it the kind of feel and substance that you like. This will then become your talisman.

Keep your talisman safe. The alchemists talk about making your Philosopher's Stone, and this is one small example of what that might be. It represents something of your essence.

You can also make a different talisman to help you focus your will on a new project. Using the set of six meanings given below as a basis, decide which of the profiles would be best for the kind of energy and application needed. Hold it and look at it just before you begin this project, and bring your sense of direction to mind.

Remember: one should not be too superstitious about talismans, or credit them with too much power. They are in the end a crystallisation of your own energies, and may or may not connect you to something greater.

Interpretation of Coloured Diagonals

- Black – your direction is towards the inner mysteries.
- Red – you are thoroughly engaged with life in all its interest and diversity.
- Gold – you want to transform what you have, and seek eternity.

A direction towards the left (from bottom right towards top left) suggests a tendency to go inwards, or back into the past. A direction towards the right (from bottom left towards top right) suggests an urge to push forward into the future. Here are some suggested analyses for each of the six types.

- Black – left: shows a drive to penetrate the inmost parts of your work and life. You leave no stone unturned, and if you find an offender, you will bring them to justice. You take nothing on face value, and want to check everything for yourself.
- Black – right: you are something of a dark horse; you like to bring power and insight into a situation, but to hide from others where you yourself stand. Beware of putting out too much negative energy. You are willing to tackle jobs that no one else wants to do.
- Red – left: your energy is very focused. You like decisive action, and to make it as precise as possible. You are also rather unpredictable, though when you do act you are absolutely committed to it. Sexuality is very important to you.
- Red – right: you are optimistic, cheerful, and sometimes extravagant. You are a lover of life, and always up for a party or social gathering. You love the company of others and joint activities, avoiding solitary projects. You are not very reliable.
- Gold – left: you try to find meaning in whatever you do, and avoid routine work. You are always looking for the magic in life, and if you find a project that appeals to you, you will put an enormous amount into it. You enjoy wit and humour.
- Gold – right: you want to spread enlightenment. You teach, write or communicate somehow to the world at large. You aren't always able to see other people's point of view because you are too enamoured of your own. You are creative, and lively.

The Stone is projected onto the land, and exalted in the mountains,
and lives in the air, and feeds in the river, that is, Mercury.

Chapter Twelve

●●●●●●●●●●●●●●●●●

Making Gold
Wherever, Whenever

There is a saying: 'When you think the work is over, that's when it *really* begins.' This emblem shows us, rather surprisingly, that not just *one* alchemical stone is to be created, but a whole galaxy of them – we can see them flying through the air, strewn on the ground and floating in the water. The 'Philosopher's Stone' has a complex relationship with gold in the alchemical tradition. But without going too far into technicalities, the image signifies that the goal of alchemy is not just to create that gold once, but to take the transformation process one stage further and 'multiply' gold all around.

Unfortunately, the secret of doing this is not found in any one formula. What works once may never work in exactly the same way again, as I discovered all too clearly one day. I'd got up very early in order to drive to an exhibition where I was working. I'd had very little sleep and, because business was slow, I found it practically impossible to stay awake as I sat there waiting for customers. But then I found a different way of handling this. I discovered that there was a point on the border just between sleeping and waking where I could enter another state of consciousness altogether. I had to try to balance there, because the moment I slipped off balance, I either began to doze or else 'woke up' to the discomfort of being tired and bored. But when I could glide through that gateway, I felt refreshed, alive and truly conscious. Surely, I told myself, I had discovered the secret of creating a kind of internal gold.

Well, of course, simply telling myself that put an end to the experience. Once we put words or labels on something, it tends to disappear completely. And although the experience was a very real one, I soon found that I could not repeat the formula in exactly the same way. Sure, that entry point to a higher state of consciousness still exists, and it can often be found between sleeping and waking, as many teachings suggest. But it doesn't work automatically. Every moment brings different conditions, and requires a different approach, a different balance. So this is why there are no set recipes in alchemy, only guidelines. In everyday alchemy, we learn about the kinds of tools we can use. Work, exercises and observation give us a storehouse of experience to guide us. But every situation is different. And, after all, that's what it means to be creative.

There is a story about a king who lived on a mountain long, long ago. He was a good and wise king, and he thought more about his people's welfare than his own. One thought troubled him above all others. 'What can I leave my people?' he asked himself. 'When I'm gone, maybe the next ruler won't be so concerned about them. What can I do that will really make a difference?'

He took himself high up into the mountains to reflect. As he sat there alone on the mountainside, and gazed down upon his kingdom below he thought: 'Perhaps I can leave them a treasure house full of wealth that will sustain them through hard times. But no – one day that will be used up.' And then he thought, 'Perhaps I can gather together all the wisdom that different people in our kingdom possess – all the ideas, all the secrets of crafts, and all the deepest insights of philosophy. That way, they will have a treasure house that can survive famine and hard times.' But that too did not satisfy him. 'Even that will die away, because new generations won't understand the ways of the old. Our words will be lost.'

And then it came to him. 'What I will do,' he decided, 'is to leave them the way to knowledge. Nobody can take that away from them.'

This is what he did. And the story also says that this is what has come down to us, through generation after generation. It is taught in different ways, in different languages. Words are never enough to describe it, though they will do for a while. It does not depend upon outward form, though it must take on a form to be understood.

Systems have to be re-invented for the time and place that we live in. It is a way for those who want to find knowledge for themselves, and who have the courage to create anew. Knowledge is always there, waiting to be tapped.

The legacy of the king on the mountain is with us today.

The Secrets of Gold

In alchemy, if you follow the work through, and are willing to undergo the process of transformation, you can develop the ability to transform the world around you. You can also open the doorway to knowledge for others. The three guidelines to follow are: observation, attention and experience. These will never fail you. To pay attention means to be aware of what is going on – behind you, above you and below you, not just in front of your eyes. And of course, you'll know by now that this applies to your inner world, not only to external space, since alchemy works in different dimensions at once. To observe means that you take note of what you see, you follow sequences, and you record what actually happens, not what you think should happen, nor what others tell you has happened. As for experience, we all have this, but in alchemy it is a touchstone. Teachings may guide you, but your experience will be the truth of the transformation process. When observation and attention are also brought into play, then you are able to know the experience for what it is, unedited and unembroidered. This builds up first of all confidence, and then faith.

Gradually, the process of transformation will change your own being, as the potential gold is released and transmuted in you. Over the course of time, this will also affect the conditions around you, and the effect that you yourself have upon people. Your gold will call forth gold in others. True, it may also cause a reaction from the dark primal material, so that you could get a negative response from some people, not just sweetness and light! Remember, though, that 'the sun and its shadow' only help to define the space. Alchemy is not about drastically polarised notions of good and evil, ignorance and enlightenment. Even these poles are only relative; we've seen how the harmonious dance of three springs out of the duality of two. Be ready, like Hermes, to tread with a light foot. He brings humour and mischief to life, elements which are just as necessary as solemnity and serious endeavour. Nimbleness, flexibility and even irreverence are needed for this work.

Alchemists are self-starters, doggedly persistent, ready to swim against the tide and not to take anything for gospel until they've discovered it for themselves. The work of transformation that you undertake will change you. It won't turn you into a superior enlightened being overnight – and maybe never at all – but the process of transformation *will* begin in your soul. It *will* change you, and for better, not for worse.

Gold stands for truth, consciousness and eternity. This is recognised by everyone at some level, sometimes unconsciously, even though the 'spiritual gold' can be confused with material wealth. In the universe there is a great cycle, the in-and-out breath of creativity. Maybe there is some truth in the old alchemical notion that gold is always evolving from the dark chaos of the primal material. Even though we don't share those traditional views of the physical nature of the universe, there is a sense in which it is true on the greater scale of creation.

The Cosmic impulse descends from the highest, divine level to the material earthly world, taking on form and substance as it does so. This is absolutely within the nature of things. In alchemical terms, this means that the eternal essence of gold came into creation and took on denser and darker forms as it became manifest, until only the seed of gold remained buried in the primal material. This is similar to the story of the king's son sent to seek for the hidden pearl, which we encountered in Chapter 1. Alchemy itself does not deal too much with this first half of the creative cycle; our starting point in alchemy is to find that seed of gold, release its potential, and transmute it back to gold, thus creating the second half of the Cosmic cycle. We thus gain wings to fly, spiritually, and may become witnesses to some of those secrets of creation.

The process goes on in an everyday way too. I used to run a shop that sold vintage clothes, and I would go off on expeditions to seek them out. I discovered that the best places of all were the old rag mills up in Yorkshire, in the north of England. Here was where old clothes came to die. The mills were semi-derelict, filthy and smelly. But they were staffed with cheerful women who laughed and joked all day, and if they liked you, would save you the kind of thing you were after. I found all kinds of 1930s and 40s treasures there, and sometimes even clothes from the Victorian era. The real eye-opener for me was that here nothing was lost – everything could be reclaimed. This was, if you like, the primal material of clothes and textiles. The mill received discarded bags and bales from jumble sales, house clearances, even from dustbins. Everything made its way up country, sold by weight and changing hands for very little money. The ladies who worked there had the job of sorting these back out into useful categories. On the vast floors of the mills, lay heaps of clothing awaiting despatch: headscarves for Nigeria, waistcoats for Pakistan, crimplene dresses for the local markets, and what they called the 'hippy gear' for people like me. On the woollens floor, everything was sorted by colour, so that heaps of gold, scarlet, emerald and blue turned the room into a kind of Aladdin's Cave of colour. All these were going to be re-spun into second-grade yarn. The only kind of material that they could not recycle was suiting – and that went to make cardboard. Sometimes I found pristine clothing there, cashmere sweaters, and embroidered blouses that had never been worn. Often, though, I had to drive a car home full of malodorous black plastic sacks, which I would decant into our garage and process through the washing machine as quickly as possible.

So the clothes of different decades, each with their own complex history of design, manufacture and use, were all discarded, sinking lower and lower in the chain. Their appeal had been lost, their value become almost negligible. But in this unattractive, discarded and often disgusting primal material, the seeds of new life could be found. Every one of these items could be reclaimed and redeemed. Even those torn or worn beyond salvation could be pulped for paper.

There are many similar ways in which we can see the cycle of creation at work. This cycle happens as much in the spiritual world as it does in the material one. In fact, one could say that every religious impulse finally becomes material. Think of the vast number of commercial enterprises that have now sprung out of the spiritual 'New Age' impulse. Money changes hands for crystals, books, magical instruments and talismans, tarot readings, rainbow robes and shamanistic workshops; and anything else that takes your fancy can be yours, if you have the cash. This is natural. This book that I am writing now will go from intangible thoughts in my brain to be transmitted through my fingers, and will appear as words on my computer. It will be printed and bound, then sold as an item in a shop. Everything inevitably takes a form, and participates in the material world. But the danger is that we only see the form, and forget its origin. We can become bogged down at the level of materiality. Alchemy is a call to wake up, to find the seeds of gold within the everyday world, and help them to grow into new gold which will have a reality on both the physical and the transcendent level. We have to care for the material, and cherish the spiritual.

Nothing can be kept absolutely pure and immaterial once it has entered the cycle of creation. But this is in keeping with the work of creation itself, which constantly renews the universe. Ultimately, as each new impulse sinks into the earth like rain, the earth is fertilised by it, and new possibilities arise from it. We have to keep faith with that cycle, and trust both its outward path from spirit to matter, and its return to the source of creation. At the pause between the out breath and the new in breath it may seem that all has disappeared. I began writing this chapter at the time of the winter solstice, when light descends into darkness. But at that very moment of utter darkness, the light is reborn. Human history has given us the knowledge of this cycle; we can have faith that the light is being re-generated, and that the days will grow in length. This knowledge brings joy, and joy is given expression in the colourful celebration of the winter festival with fresh greenery, fire, music and parties. Of course, in the Christian Church, the winter festival has become the great feast of Christmas, the birth of the child of light. At this time, we affirm human love, give presents to seal those bonds and renew contact those who are far away. Rituals and festivals are a collective form of 'gold-making'.

I have been revising the last few pages of this book during a short trip to Russia, working in my room on the sixteenth floor of a Moscow hotel. Just as I was recalling the story of the 'Hymn of the Robe of Glory', and the eagle that flew to the king's son as a messenger, I suddenly became aware that a bird had flown in through my own window. It was a blue tit or *sinitsa* – a 'little bluebird', as it is known in Russian. Russia is now frozen in the depths of winter, and the ground is covered with snow; birds are few and far between. In addition, the room is very high up and the window was open only a crack and covered by lace curtains. So how did the bird get in so easily, without my noticing? (Luckily, I was soon able persuade it to fly out again.) Coincidence? Maybe – but it was certainly a reminder to me that this is a living tradition, not just words on the page. Alchemy is a kind of dialogue with the universe; we are a part of the living world that we inhabit. The messenger bird may be as ready to fly to us today if we evoke its presence.

There was more to come. When I had written this short account of the 'bluebird', I put on my heavy sheepskin coat and snow boots, and went out to the market to do some shopping. On my return, I started to empty out my bags on the bed, and a gold ring tumbled out! I couldn't believe my eyes. I thought it had to be something made of base metal, but when I looked at it closely, I saw that it was a hall-marked gold wedding ring. It is one thing to write about the alchemical search for gold, and quite another to have some gold fall unexpectedly out of your shopping bag. There is usually a 'rational' explanation for such strange events, which 'explains' how they came about. In this case, a stallholder probably dropped her ring accidentally as she helped me to pack up my purchases – and I'll do my best to find her and return it. But in my experience, the mundane explanation doesn't make these 'epiphanies' any less extraordinary. The universe is responsive to our output, and there is a kind of two-way communication. This is what the alchemists have always known.

Exercise 1: Epiphanies

Be on the lookout for any unusual appearances or 'epiphanies' that come your way. They may have a mundane cause (i.e. they have a cause in the physical world, and are not miracles), but they will also be both symbolic and full of resonance. They have 'meaning', but not necessarily a meaning that you can pin down with one interpretation. If something like this occurs, let it speak to you on its own terms. Or, if you can remember something similar from the past, look at it from your current perspective. What significance does it have for you now?

Sacred Space

You have the tools that this book has given you. Now you need to have faith in them, and apply them. However, there is one last kind of exercise that I would like to leave you with. This is done with the intention of enlivening the space around you. The technique I'm about to suggest creates an arena for action and interaction. It sets up a space for the multiplication of gold, as the alchemists call it.

As you might expect, there is no sure-fire automatic way to do this. The best we can do is to use a helpful framework, focus our intention, and put ourselves in an attentive frame of mind. Something will usually change and become more alive as a result, at the very least, but it can never be absolutely guaranteed.

The approach I use for this is known as 'The Magic Lantern'. It consists of creating an imaginary sphere in which you can stand. It can also be drawn out as an octahedron, using straight lines instead of curved, which will give you a more lantern-like shape. However, for practical purposes, you will probably find the spherical version easier to use. You can use the Magic Lantern in any context where you wish for the best possible outcome, irrespective of your own personal desires and wishes. Where could this apply? Examples could be in ritual and ceremony of any kind, or if you are working as a healer or therapist, or in performance, or as a starting point for a meditation practice. I have found it a wonderful framework to use for singing and for giving lectures, and it would be equally suitable for acting, story-telling, concerts or any other kind of performance. But before taking it into your chosen context, I suggest that you practise setting up the Magic Lantern on your own.

Exercise 2: The Magic Lantern

Do this in a room which a reasonable amount of space in it. Stand in the centre of the room, and imagine a transparent sphere extending outwards all around you, encompassing everything that you can see. You are standing at the centre of the sphere. Breathe deeply and easily, and encourage the sphere to expand to its full extent.

Become aware that your solar plexus marks the exact centre of the sphere, and that this is the point through which three axes pass. Give the solar plexus some attention; it has some substance to it, which you may perhaps feel as warmth, or light.

Now imagine a line extending from the top of your sphere down through the solar plexus and beyond to the bottom of the sphere. Be aware that even though the sphere you have constructed is limited in size, the line itself could continue to infinity. This vertical line represents Heaven and the Underworld. It connects the highest, most refined consciousness with the powerful instincts and forces of the depths below.

Then imagine a line that starts behind you, and passes through the solar plexus out to the front of your sphere (again, this line is really infinite). This represents your own outer and inner worlds. It can be the physical world that greets your senses out front, as opposed to the inner world of your thoughts and feelings, which stretches behind you into the unconscious. Another way of looking at it, especially useful in performance, is to see the forward line as connecting you with the

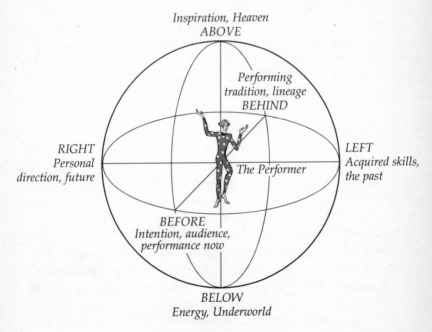

Inspiration, Heaven
ABOVE

Performing
tradition, lineage
BEHIND

RIGHT
Personal
direction, future

The Performer

LEFT
Acquired skills,
the past

BEFORE
Intention, audience,
performance now

BELOW
Energy, Underworld

THE MAGIC LANTERN
(A performer's version, which can be adapted for ritual or sacred work)

audience, and the backward line linking you with the tradition of performance which you are following.

Finally, bring in the third line, which runs horizontally from left to right. You now have three lines or axes intersecting at the point of the solar plexus. This last line represents your past (left) and your future (right). It can be seen as your pilgrimage through life.

And so you have brought together different dimensions of space and time. You are centred, but you have extended the world beyond the limits of your personal concerns. If you use the Magic Lantern where there are other people present, make sure that sphere really expands to include everyone. Although your known world literally ends with the floor or ground beneath your feet, with practice you will find it easy to extend your sphere well below this point, emphasising the idea of the 'Underworld' below. By trying this out in practice, you will find what kind of size sphere you need to use in different contexts, neither so large that you lose contact with it, nor too small and restricting. A good rule of thumb is to extend it as far as you can see and a little further. The sphere itself is always transparent, so that any good influences created within it may pass through it to the world beyond. It is *not* the same as 'sealing' or protecting a room, which blocks that space off from outside contacts.

Find a moment before the action really starts to set up your Magic Lantern. It will help you to become centred and focused. You can use it even if you are not the chief protagonist – you can be a humble member of a large choir, or a participant in a celebration with hundreds of other people, and still set up the Magic Lantern. You can, if you wish, make a dedication or a statement of intent when the sphere and its axes are first in place. This can be silent, and it should be brief, reduced to its essential components. Work it out carefully first, and beware of imposing your own limiting desires on the event.

Once the performance, practice or ritual is under way, you can trust the Magic Lantern to stay in place; you don't need to keep re-affirming it, although you may like to bring it to mind now and then. You will only find out by experience what kind of a difference it makes. But the chances are that when you create space for the sacred, you may also help to create gold in the world around you.

Good luck!

Appendices

• • • • • • • • • • • • • •

1. Group Work
• •

Groups are welcome to use the material from this book as a basic course struc-
ture. However, acknowledgement of this book must be given both to its
members and in any related publicity.

These few notes are brief suggestions, and not a complete guide to
group work. Nowadays, many people have experience in running
groups of all kinds, and there is plenty of good advice to be found in
manuals and practical courses elsewhere. Here are some basic guidelines
which should be enough to provide a secure foundation for the work:

The minimum recommended number for a working group is
seven people. This is because seven people begin to constitute a
'common mind'. Individuality and personal responsibility is not lost,
but a collective pool of ideas and energies can form, which gives the
group a greater consciousness and a proper potential for receiving
knowledge.

With fewer than seven people, the group will be predominantly a
collection of individuals, and differences of opinion, clashes of
personality, and so on, will be far more evident. Any number of individuals can of course meet and report to one another, but the effects
will be different.

Useful ground rules for group work are:

- Leave your personality outside the door.
- No criticism of oneself or others.
- Neither accept nor reject.

A group needs a leader. This person has the responsibility of keeping a
watch over the whole, of tuning into the general response and energy

without getting lost in his or her own dreams and fancies. Sometimes he or she may have to step back mentally from an exercise in order to monitor it. This is particularly relevant to visualisation, where the leader must ask questions to bring out images lurking on the edge of consciousness, or steer the visualisation back onto solid ground when it gets bogged down.

The leader does not have to be wiser than the others, but he or she should be a stable person with reasonable control of his or her personality, so that there will be no sudden uncontrolled bursts of temper or flights of fancy, which can seriously damage the delicate psyche of the group. The psyche of a group in session is in many ways like the innocent, eager and vulnerable mind of a child – wide open to possibilities, and capable of experiencing shock and hurt if attacked.

It is possible to change the leader at intervals, but being over-democratic and allowing everybody a turn is not a good idea. There may be people who are not really suited to the role, and too many different flavours can spoil the soup. There is no especial kudos attached to being a leader, because this person is doing a job of work, not parading their superior enlightenment.

The leader should formally open and close the session, so that meetings end on a down-to-earth note. No one should be encouraged to wander off from the group while still 'away with the fairies'. Having something to eat and drink is a good traditional way to end a session.

Commitment is important, and is the bugbear of our present era, when we are all encouraged to sample and be finicky consumers. But, as one meditation instructor once put it: 'The only way to get to the water is to dig a deep well in one place. If you dig a little here and there, you will never find it.'

2. Michael Maier's Emblems

The alchemical images used in this book come from a collection called *Atlanta Fugiens*, written by Michael Maier and published in 1617.

Maier was a talented late-Renaissance doctor, philosopher and diplomat, as well as a poet and musician. He was also, of course, an alchemist, but one who believed in drawing all knowledge into the alchemical sphere, creating a potent microcosm in which the different strands of knowledge could interact and enliven the path to transformation. In his book, each of the 50 emblems is also accompanied by a short poem or epigram, written in Latin. More astonishingly, each one also has a three-part fugue, with words and music to be sung by three voices. Maier instructed us to read, sing, listen and meditate at the same time – and 'not without a certain pleasure'! To do this from beginning to end of his remarkable work would be a course of instruction in itself. However, although we can't follow that path here, I have chosen Maier's emblems as a basis for our own course as they are vivid and evocative, and they illuminate so much about the work of transformation.

Those who would like to follow Maier's alchemical tale can find a full translation, with excellent notes by Joscelyn Godwin and an accompanying cassette of the music published by Magnum Opus Hermetic Sourceworks 22, Phanes Press 1989.

3. Alchemical Definitions

Salt, Mercury and Sulphur

These are the names alchemists give to the three principles which underlie everything in creation. They are not literally the chemical substances of salt, mercury and sulphur, but stand as symbols for the active forces of life, which must be unpicked and realigned during the alchemical process. Salt is stable and incombustible, while mercury is subtle and volatile, and sulphur is bright with fiery light. Maier chose to weave these three principles into his book by using the story of Atlanta, Hippomenes and the Golden Apple. In this classical tale, the huntress Atlanta is pursued by the youth Hippomenes, who hopes to overtake her in a race so that she will consent to marry him. He throws down three golden apples, which distract her enough for him to catch up with her. In Maier's version, the fleeing Atlanta stands for the 'fugitive' mercury, Hippomenes is fiery sulphur, and the golden apples represent the salt of the alchemical operation. These give the three lines of his musical fugues that accompany the emblems.

The three principles also stand for body, soul and spirit. In alchemy, even a physical substance is considered to have a soul and a spirit as well as a body. One problem is how exactly to attribute soul and spirit to mercury and sulphur. It depends also on how you define soul and spirit. Salt is easy; everyone is agreed that it stands for the body and materiality. I am following the tradition that defines the spirit as eternal, and supra-personal, and the soul as that which binds body and spirit together. This means that in this book, mercury stands for the soul, and sulphur the spirit.

The Symbols of Alchemy

The language of alchemy *is* symbol and image. Through these, the subtle and elusive teaching of alchemy is conveyed; alchemy works on the imagination, and at a deeper level these symbols speak to us about transformation, and about the way we as human beings are connected into life. Symbols are heralds, portents and cross-cultural messengers, and as such touch us deeply even if we cannot always analyse their meaning exactly.

Anyone who wishes to make a comprehensive study of alchemical symbolism faces a lifetime's work. Symbols have evolved, multiplied and changed over the long course of alchemy, and every writer and illustrator has found their own way of using the imagery. Most of the images I have used in this book, such as the red and green lion, and the serpent Ouroboros, can be found in core alchemical sources, and I have drawn on their basic accepted meanings. However, like any other writer on alchemy, I've developed them according to my own understanding and experience. Alchemy is based on experience, and so each person who uses and interprets alchemical symbolism is contributing to the evolution of alchemy.

The symbols of alchemy are immediate, graphic, sometimes raw, and often colourful or dramatic. Some of them are drawn from the properties of the materials that alchemists worked with, so that, for instance, a grey wolf stands for antimony, and a black crow for lead. Some relate to accepted correspondences, especially from Medieval and Renaissance times, in which, for example, sun = gold = king = lion = golden flower, and so on. However, colouring could change that, so that although a green lion and a red lion represent nature and energy, and water and fire, they are early versions of the refined golden lion, so to speak.

The great personal visions of leading alchemists, such as those of Zosimos in the fourth century AD who saw a 'man of copper' and a temple of alabaster, also provided material for later alchemists to use, and they thus have their own frame of reference. Alchemists liked to tread in the steps of the masters, and often built on earlier symbolic revelations. They would also draw from traditions linked to alchemy, such as astrology, since metals and planets were linked in alchemy. Sometimes this was used in a more self-conscious way, so that seven sons, steps or stars in an alchemical emblem might represent the seven planets and their metals.

Decoding alchemical symbolism can be complex, because sometimes it is based on personal revelation, sometimes on the current symbolism of the time, and sometimes on classical mythology, Christianity or parallel traditions such as Kabbalah. In general, the earlier Medieval illustrations and texts are simpler and more direct in their use of symbolism, whereas the learned scholar-alchemists of the sixteenth and seventeenth centuries were more likely to use an overlay of symbolism and allusions from other sources, and to create a puzzle for the head as well as for the imagination.

As well as using imagery graphically, it was also common to create a symbolic structure for an alchemical text. One of the most famous is *The Twelve Gates* of George Ripley, in which each 'gate' equals a stage of alchemy, and the whole is likened to a castle with 12 entrances. This resonates with other sources of symbolism, such as the 12 gates of the Holy City in the Bible. Alchemy contains both the carefully presented structure of spiritual philosophy, and the unpredictable dynamism and drama of a dream. Its symbolism is a unique mixture of the two.

The Alchemical Process

Each alchemist described the process of transformation differently. Some said there were seven stages, some 12, and they did not agree on the exact order in which these took place. They used terms that are now obscure, such as *calcination*, *congelation*, and *cibation*. Rather than giving a precise ordering of the stages, which would only be one version among many, I would prefer to indicate just a general outline of the alchemical process.

The Prime Material is sought, and is to be found as some kind of base substance, which might be in the earth, in excrement, as a metallic deposit or else be something generally overlooked. It contains the seeds of gold, or the possibility of evolving into gold. An egg is a common symbol for this, as is Ouroboros, the dragon with its tail in its mouth. The material must then be purified, often both by heating and by washing. It has to be divided, split open in such a way as to release the two polarised forms of energy which it contains. These can be shown as dog and wolf, two fighting lions or other combatants. The symbols for these can then be brought into a new and charged union, symbolised by male and female or king and queen, but the result of that union, shown as a newborn child, must then die. This is the stage of 'putrefaction' or 'nigredo', as the substance blackens and decays. Often a black raven or crow is the image used for this. Then the refined 'soul' rises from the dead material and is distilled into a higher form of matter. This must be concentrated down again into a recognisable form and substance, and nourished so that it grows. It is now ready to become gold, having completed the gamut of metallic evolution. This can be shown as sun and moon, and the resurrected golden king with his silver queen. But to be fully potent it must be 'fermented' and 'exalted', so that it becomes the essence of gold. In this state, it is known as the Elixir, or the Philosopher's Stone. Now, when it is 'projected' onto fresh Primal Material, it can turn that too into gold.

In *Everyday Alchemy* I have broadly followed this outline, paying particular attention both to Maier's emblems, and to the sequence laid out by George Ripley in his *Compound of Alchemy, Containing Twelve Gates* (included in *Theatrum Chemicum Britannicum*, Elias Ashmole). Like anyone working in the alchemical tradition, I have also developed my own understanding and interpretation of this sequence. The Great Work, as the path of alchemical transformation is known, is created anew every time, but it is founded on certain principles and these must be learnt and passed on to others for the work to flower.

Contact Addresses

• •

Here are the details of some recommended groups and organisations for meditation and other transformational work:

High Peak Meditation
UK: PO Box 34, Todmorden, OL14 8XB
USA: c/o R. Smoley, Lindisfarne Books, PO Box 799, Great Barrington, MA 01230,
Australia: e-mail: meunna@msn.com.au
Website: www.highpeakmeditation.co.uk
Offers one-to-one guidance in a non-denominational meditation, with residential courses to augment daily practice.

Samatha Meditation
The Samatha Centre
Green Street
Llangullo
Nr Knighton
Powys LD7 1SP
UK
Website: www.samatha.org
A Buddhist practice based on attention to the breath; taught in the West for over 40 years. Groups around the UK.

The Saros Tradition
Saros London
119 Dollis Park
London N3 1BT
UK
A tradition of knowledge through philosophy and meditation.

SpaceCentre
72 Leathwaite Rd
London SW11 6RT
UK
E-mail: Briarmax@72aol.com
Movements based on the evolution of vertebrates to explore the relationship between inner and outer, higher and lower.

The Way of the Charcoal Burner
105 Middleton Hall Rd
Kings Norton
Birmingham B30 1AG
UK
E-mail: enquiries@sareoso.org
Practical/adventure courses working with attention and using ancient traditions & techniques.

Working at the Edge
30a Shepherds Hill
Highgate
London N6 5AH
www.ynysprydein.org
Exploring the Otherworld through the British Native Tradition. London-based group.

Select Bibliography

Primary Sources

Gilchrist, C. *The Elements of Alchemy*, Element Books, Shaftesbury, UK, 1991.

Maier, M. *Atlanta Fugiens*, trans. Joscelyn Godwin, Phanes Press, USA, 1989.

Source Books for Alchemical Texts

Ashmole, E. *Theatrum Chemicum Britannicum*, 1651: facsimile edition Kessinger Publishing Co., USA (no date).

Trismosin, S. *Splendor Solis*, trans. Joscelyn Godwin, Phanes Press, USA, 1991.

Waite, A.E. (ed.) *The Hermetic Museum 1652*, Samuel Weiser, Inc., USA, 1991.

Books on Alchemy

Haeffner, M. *A Dictionary of Alchemy*, Aquarian Press, London, 1991.

Holmyard, E.J. *Alchemy*, original edition Penguin Books, London, 1957.

Klossowski de Rola, S. *The Golden Game*, Thames & Hudson, London, 1988.

Sherwood Taylor, F. *The Alchemists*, Paladin, London, 1976.

Related Traditions

Brown, N. *Hermes the Thief*, Lindisfarne Press, USA, 1990.

Gilchrist, C. and Zur, G. *The Tree of Life Oracle*, forthcoming, Eddison Sadd, London; Barnes & Noble, USA.

Oliver, L. *The Meditator's Guidebook*, Destiny Books, USA, 1991.

Wilde, L. Webster, *Working with your Dreams*, Blandford, UK, 1995.

Acknowledgements

* *

I am very grateful to Joscelyn Godwin for permission to use his translations of Maier's epigrams, which are taken from:

> *Michael Maier's Atlanta Fugiens*, translated and edited by Joscelyn Godwin, Phanes Press, USA, 1989

I would also like to thank my editor, Susan Lascelles, for her helpful support and thoughtful suggestions. We first met during unseasonably snowy weather in March 2001, on a day when my car had broken down and her route home threatened to be cut off; the difficulties concentrated our minds wonderfully and from out of that meeting *Everyday Alchemy* was born.

Thanks also go to Doreen Montgomery, who has also been as much of a friend as an agent, and who has encouraged me to keep going through thick and thin.

I would also like to acknowledge the age-old tradition of alchemy for which, much to my surprise, my services as a spokeswoman have been required on a number of occasions. I hope I do it justice, and that I contribute in some measure to the ever-changing Hermetic line of knowledge.

Index

∙∙∙∙∙∙∙∙